Date Due

THE CANUCK BOOK

Ian Walker   Keith Bellows

With illustrations by Graham Pilsworth

General Publishing Co. Limited, Don Mills, Ontario

First published 1977 by
General Publishing Co. Limited
30 Lesmill Road
Don Mills, Ontario

First printing

Canadian Cataloguing in Publication Data

Walker, Ian F.
   The Canuck Book
ISBN 0-7736-1039-1
1. Canada — Miscellanea. I. Bellows, Keith.
II. Title.
FC60.W34   971'.002   C78-001066-3
F1008.W34

Design/Peter Maher

Quality paperback ISBN 0-7736-1039-1
Printed and bound in Canada

To our wives who provided
much criticism — as usual.

TABLE OF CONTENTS

With special thanks to the ferrets: Andy
Caddell, Horst Dornbusch, David Dunbar,
Frances Mullen, Bonnie Bellows, Kevin, Bob
and Gladys Walker; to Frank Sixt, for the legal
advice; and to Pat and Nancy.

ADVERTISING

Perhaps the most successful ad campaign in Canadian history was created in 1954 by the Quaker Oats Company when it dreamed up a scheme to give away part of Canada — by the square inch. To boost its sagging sales the company purchased 19 acres of land near Dawson, Yukon Territory, and formed the Klondike Big Inch Land Co. The acres were then divided into 21 million square-inch lots, and a deed for one lot was included free with every box of cereal. The response was outstanding. One youngster sent in a piece of string and four toothpicks and asked the company to erect a fence around his property. Another customer wrote that he had amassed 10,800 individual lots — and was thus entitled to 75 square feet of Yukon land (it didn't seem to bother him that the lots were scattered throughout the 19 acres). A man in Buffalo, on trial for murdering his wife with an ice pick, lost his counsel when the lawyer discovered that his client, whom he had thought to be a wealthy landowner, held only 1,000 Quaker Oats title deeds. The Big Inch Land Co. finally folded in the early '60s when the Canadian government repossessed the 19 acres for nonpayment of taxes. The amount owed — $37.20.

The highest advertising rates in Canadian publishing are those charged by *The Canadian* and *Weekend*, Canada's top-selling general-interest magazines. *The Canadian*, with a circulation of 1,980,000, charges a national rate of $22,960 for a four-color, full-page ad. *Weekend*, with a circulation of 1,714,000, charges $20,265.

The world's loftiest advertising signs are atop the Bank of Montreal's 935-foot-high First Canada Place in Toronto. There are four displays, each 20 by 22 feet.

Canada's biggest advertising sign belongs to Hiram Walker distillery. The 13,407-square-foot sign is on the distillery's grain elevators in Walkerville, Ontario.

Canadian companies are surprisingly honest in their advertising. A recent survey indicated that 50 percent of products gave the advertised quantity, 38 percent gave more and only 12 percent gave less than promised.

The longest-running show on Broadway wasn't a theater production. It was the 50-by-62-foot Canadian Club sign that illuminated — with 4,000 light bulbs and five miles of neon tubing — New York's Times Square for almost 24 years. That's three times longer than the longest-running Broadway theater production (*Fiddler on the Roof*, 1964-72: 3,242 performances). The Canadian Club sign, sad to say, was retired in January 1977.

AGRICULTURE

Canada's first farmer was Louis Hébert, a Paris-born apothecary who tilled the land near Port Royal, Nova Scotia, in 1606. His son-in-law Guillaume Couillard was reputedly the first man in Canada to use a plow.

Western Canada's first field of wheat was seeded in 1754 in Saskatchewan's Carrot River valley. The sower's name: Chevalier de la Corne.

The Valley of the Jolly Green Giant is actually near Tecumseh, Ontario, about ten miles east of Windsor. And for anyone who cares: actor Len Dressler was the original voice of the giant, and Colorado skier Keith Wagman was the first to portray him on television.

The world's largest known wheat field, planted in 1951 near Lethbridge, Alberta, was more than 35,000 acres — about twice the size of Bermuda. But then the world's biggest breadbasket *is* the Prairies.

The first rust-resistant wheat in Canada was developed in 1804 by David Fife, an Ontario farmer. And while we can't tell you his formula, we can let you in on an 1884 patent for making *gold* from wheat: Cut the wheat into fine snippets, put the pieces in cold water for ten hours at 15°C, then strain the liquid into a china dish and let it stand for 24 hours. According to Harry Fell, the man who dreamed up the process, the surface skim will be gold.

The world's largest hayfield is at Tantramar Marshes near Sackville, New Brunswick. It covers an area of almost 90 square miles.

Canada's largest farm? Well, the natives of Prince Edward Island call their verdant province "The Million-Acre Farm." Actually the island is 3,584,000 acres — most of which is cultivated. The largest farm on P.E.I. is Webster's, at the eastern tip.

The first cultivated tree fruit in Canada was the apple. In 1633 Pierre Martin grew apples at Annapolis Royal, Nova Scotia; the first commercial cultivation of apples took place in the nearby Annapolis Valley.

The world's first McIntosh apple tree died in Dundela, Ontario, in 1905 at the ripe old age of 95. By way of eulogy, we'd like to remind you of some other North American apples available in Canada: Baldwin, Bancroft, Ben Davis, Bishops' Pippin, Cortland, Duchess, Golden Delicious, Gravenstein, Grimes Golden, Jonathan, Joyce, Kendall, Lobo, Lodi, Macoun, Maiden Blush, Melba, Milton, Northern Spy, Northwestern Greening, Rambo, Rome Beauty, Red Duchess, Secor, Spartan, Spice Russet, Spitzenberg, Stayman Winesap, Wealty, Williams Red, Yellow Newton, Yellow Transplant and York Imperial . . . .

An apple tree produces not only fruit but enough oxygen in its lifetime to supply a human for four years. In that time he inhales and exhales more than 33 million times and breathes in more than 25 tons of oxygen.

The world's largest squash was grown in Roland, Manitoba, in 1971. It tipped the scales at 353 pounds — about the weight of a side of beef.

The world's largest wooden oxcart is at Selkirk, Manitoba. It's 22 feet high and 45 feet long. And the ox to pull the cart? It would weigh about two tons. The second-largest wooden oxcart in the world, 25 feet long and 10 feet high, is at Oak Lake, Manitoba.

ANIMALS

The only turtle to go over Niagara Falls and survive was called Sonny Boy. The turtle, accompanied by George Stathakis — a flamboyant mystic who claimed to be 1,000 years old — made the trip in a 2,000-pound barrel in 1930. Unfortunately the barrel was dragged behind a cataract and held under the ceaseless torrent for 22 hours. When the barrel was rescued and the lid pried open, Stathakis had suffocated. As for Sonny Boy — well, he survived but was kidnapped a few months later at an exhibition.

Canada's biggest turtle derby is held each August at Boissevain, Manitoba, the "Land of Tommy Turtle." The race features more than a hundred hard-shelled competitors, all vying for the world championship. A recent winner was Spike, a Canadian entry who crawled away from a weak bid by Jimmy, a U.S. competitor. Despite a stirring pre-race blast over the PA system of "Stars and Stripes Forever," Jimmy not only lost — he never even moved. Jimmy's handler had an explanation: his turtle thought he was in a "stone" race, when in fact the event was a "flat" race. It seems in a stone race, *last* off the mark wins.

Canada's biggest frog, which lived in the 1880s, weighed 42 pounds. It was raised by its owner on a diet of whiskey, bugs and buttermilk — but finally croaked when someone dynamited near its pond at Killarney Lake, New Brunswick. Its stuffed remains are in the York-Sunbury Museum at Fredericton.

The Canadian Frog Jumping Championship, incidentally, is held each August at St. Pierre, Manitoba.

A recently issued Canadian Wildlife Service brochure had some rather perilous advice for French-speaking campers. Entitled "What to do in the presence of polar bears," it suggested, in English, that 30 yards is a wise distance to keep between oneself and a polar bear. The French version, however, gives 30 *feet* as "une distance prudente."

The wildlife people aren't trying to turn francophones into bear bait, however. The problem is one of modesty: the French word for yard is *verge* — and verge is slang for the male sex organ.

The world's largest bull moose was shot in the Yukon in 1897. It stood 7 feet 8 inches at the withers and weighed 1,800 pounds.

The world's most expensive cow, contrary to what many Canadians think, does not sit in the House of Commons. It chews grass outside Oakville, Ontario, and was sold in November 1976 by Claude Picket, a dairyman from Hornby, for $235,000.

Canada's biggest beaver is at Dauphin, Manitoba. The 16-foot-high sculpture is called Amisk, a Cree word for beaver.

Jumbo, the largest elephant ever held in captivity, and the biggest ever seen by modern man, was killed by a hurtling train at St. Thomas, Ontario, on September 15, 1885. The seven-ton colossus, who liked to share a snort of whiskey or a pint of beer with his trainer, Matthew Scott, belonged to circus magnate Phineas Barnum. After Jumbo's death, Barnum built two special wagons to carry and display the elephant's 1,538-pound skin and 2,400-pound, 11-foot 7-inch skeleton.

The largest stockyards in Canada are at St. Boniface, Manitoba. They can hold more than 25,000 head of cattle — or a life's supply of beef for roughly 1,800 Canadians (the average Canadian eats 14 head of cattle in a lifetime).

A world record for butterfat production was set by Springbank Snow Countess, a cow raised in Woodstock, Ontario. Between 1919 and 1936 she yielded 9,062 pounds of the stuff.

The highest-priced bull in history was "Joe's Pride," an Albertan beefalo — one quarter Hereford, three-eighths charolais and three-eights buffalo — sold in September 1974 for $2.5 million.

Canada's most unusual exercise track for horses was designed by Romeo Lebault of Oka, Quebec. It's an 11-foot-deep, 70,000-gallon swimming pool. Apparently a half-hour in the pool is the same to a horse as an 18-mile jog is to a man.

What is believed to be the largest collection of horse brasses in Canada is displayed at the Coach and Horses Gift Shop at Woodleigh, Prince Edward Island.

The first horse was brought to Canada from France in 1647. Indians reacted strangely when they first saw men on horseback: they thought the rider and the horse were a single creature.

Strange as it seems, there are no buffalos in Canada — unless they're in a zoo. Buffalo is a term that applies only to African and Asian species; Canada's species are properly called *bison*, and there aren't too many of them.

Less than two centuries ago there were an estimated 60 million bison in North America — so many that one Prairie-dweller remarked that buggy-drivers on the plains had to stop periodically to pull bisons' hooves from the spokes of the wheels. Today there are about 12,000 bison in Canada; the largest herd — about 8,000 strong — is in Wood Buffalo National Park.

Canada's fastest mammal is the pronghorn antelope, found in southern Alberta and Saskatchewan. It hits speeds of up to 60 miles an hour.

Canada's only herd of camels was brought to British Columbia in 1858 during the building of the Cariboo Trail. Frank Laumeister paid $6,000 for 28 of them on the assumption that each could carry 1,000 pounds compared to a mule's 300. What he hadn't counted on, however, was the smell. The camels stank. They stank so badly, in fact, that the mules belonging to "Dirty Harry" Strousse panicked at first whiff.

Camels were strange enough, but Laumeister went one better. The beasts had trouble traversing rocky terrain, so he fitted them all with leather shoes. The camels were kept for several years, and some escaped. The last camel-sighting in British Columbia was in 1925.

Montreal is believed to have more pets than any other Canadian city. Some 75,000 cats and dogs are destroyed annually; and the 200,000 that remain deposit about 30.3 million gallons of urine — enough to keep Niagara Falls flowing for 16 seconds — on the city streets each year. On top of that, so to speak, they deposit 36.5 million pounds of solid waste.

The heaviest load ever hauled by a dog was pulled by a Canadian dog. In July 1973 Bonzo Bear, a 162-pound Newfoundland, dragged a 4,400-pound weight a distance of more than 15 feet.

Canada's only prairie-dog town is in Frenchman Valley, Saskatchewan. Roughly 5,000 blacktailed prairie dogs (an endangered species) inhabit the underground network of tunnels and burrows.

The world's largest house cat is Boots, who lives with his owner, Mary Price, in Hamilton, Ontario. Boots weighs 53 pounds — about the weight of a fully-grown Alsatian German shepherd, and almost ten pounds more than the previous world record holder.

Canada's longest survived cat-fall took place on May 1, 1973. Gros Minou plunged 20 floors from a Montreal apartment building; she incurred only a fractured pelvis. (Of course, if she hadn't pulled through, there are an estimated 6.5 million Canadian cats that could have taken her place.)

The earliest reptiles were inhabitants of Nova Scotia: the *Protoclepsybrobs* and *Archerpeton* hung out in the Bluenose province about 290 billion years ago.

AUTOMOBILES, SNOWMOBILES & BICYCLES

The first man in Canada to own a car was Georges-Antoine Belcourt, a Prince Edward Island priest. In 1866 he took the car on its maiden spin to a Sunday school picnic. When he arrived he honked the horn, revved the engine, then crashed into a fence post. This, of course, was Canada's first car accident.

the ginger ale that came to be known as Canada Dry.

The oddest journey across Canada by car took place in 1927 when George Scott and Frank Elliot traveled from Halifax to the West Coast in a Model-T Ford. The trip took 89 days — and they didn't fill the gas tank once. Instead they cajoled 168 passing motorists into towing the vehicle. The reason? It had no engine.

Canada's first commercially built car was completed in 1908 by R. S. McLaughlin. He went on to become chairman of General Motors (Canada), and held the position until his death in 1971, shortly after his hundredth birthday. McLaughlin's brother Jack was no fizzle-out either: he invented

The first person to drive an automobile across Canada was Thomas Wilby. He set out from Halifax in a Reo Special on August 17, 1912, and reached Victoria 52 days and 4,200 miles later. Wilson carried with him a flask of Atlantic seawater, which he emptied into the Pacific.

Canada now has some 7,900,000 registered automobiles — about one for every three Canadians — which consume about 6½ million gallons of gas annually.

And if you're wondering why your car keeps breaking down, here's one possibility: the average car driven in Canada contains 15,000 separate parts, so there's lots to go wrong. More than 1½ million abandoned autos litter the Canadian landscape. If the metal from these machines was recycled, it would be worth more than $50 million.

Canada's longest car was built by U. H. Dandurand in 1898. It was 26 feet long, weighed six tons and slept 11.

The first Canadian filling station was established in June 1908 at the corner of Vancouver's Smith and Cambie streets. The pump was in the kitchen and the gas came through a garden hose.

The first Canadian to reach the North Pole by snowmobile was Jean-Luc Bombardier, nephew of Joseph-Armand Bombardier, inventor of the snowmobile. Jean-Luc's expedition took 44 days and 1 hour to cover the 413 miles between their base camp on

Ward Hunt Island and the Pole. They celebrated their arrival by sucking on frozen champagne.

In 1976 Lester Wolfe had to abandon his quest to travel 3,500 miles by snowmobile from Pickle Lake, Ontario, to Fairbanks, Alaska. After covering 2,739 miles — and losing 32 pounds — Wolfe ran out of snow.

Canada's longest jaunt on a bicycle built for three was accomplished by Jean and Nicolette Besnard and their three-year-old son Alexandre. The three-month journey, which began in Montreal on May 19, 1977, ended 2,800 miles later in Vancouver. It was the first leg of a round-the-world trip.

Canada's coast-to-coast cycling record is held by Vancouver's Wayne Phillips. He pedaled the 3,742 miles from the West Coast to Halifax's city hall in 19 days, 22 hours and 57 minutes. He beat the previous mark by four days.

AVIATION

The first airplane flight in Canada took place at Baddeck, Nova Scotia, on February 23, 1909. The plane, the *Silver Dart*, was piloted by J. A. McCurdy. It crashed on its fifth landing.

The first trans-Canada flight took place in 1920. Although the flying time was only 45 hours, the journey lasted 11 days.

Canada's busiest air route is between Montreal and Toronto: it's used by about 915,000 travelers yearly. Some 15 million passengers fly within Canada annually, and about four million fly internationally. Canada's three biggest airports — Vancouver, Toronto and Montreal — handle almost 20 million passengers each year. And 57 major Canadian airports log almost six million takeoffs and landings each year.

The largest airport in the world is Montreal's Mirabel. It covers some 90,000 acres, although at present only 17,000 acres are operational. More than 10 million passengers use the airport annually; it's projected that by 2025 almost a million passengers will use it *each week*.

Canada's first known balloon flight took place in Saint John, New Brunswick. The *Star of the East* went aloft on August 10, 1840.

The first woman in Canada to receive a pilot's license was Eileen Vollick of Hamilton, Ontario. She earned her wings in 1928.

The world's most northerly parachute jump was made in 1969 by Ray Munro of Lancaster, Ontario. He jumped above the Polar ice cap — at 87°30′N — in -39°C (-39°F) weather. Munro tumbled at speeds of up to 180 miles per hour, enough to push the wind chill factor to -176°C (-285°F).

The first Canadian to save his life with a parachute was Jack Caldwell, in 1929. Trivial to you, maybe, but not to him.

The record for Canada's highest night parachute jump is held by Bill Cole and Rick Wall of Mississauga, Ontario. In September 1976 they dropped 28,000 feet before opening their chutes and wafting to earth at Toronto International Airport.

Along with Murray Smith, Cole — Canada's only professional stunt parachutist — set the Canadian high-altitude record with a 31,000-foot jump above Camp Borden, Ontario, in –34°C (–30°F) temperatures. That dive also established the Canadian record for the longest free fall — 170 seconds.

When it comes to air travel, federal regulations are extremely down-to-earth. One law, for instance, states that no passenger is permitted to leave a craft in flight — except by parachute. But get this: it's also forbidden to enter a plane while it's in flight!

Canadian Aviation magazine wins our most dubious writing award for this paragraph on the Snowbirds, the Canadian Armed Forces Acrobatic Team: "Later, in the 409 squadron briefing room, the Snowbirds reviewed their performance from startup to shut-down. Debriefing was accomplished with short, sharp ejaculations and a lot of hand movements. The men were not happy with what they had done."

Canada's first air hijacking occurred on September 11, 1968, when Charles Beasely of Dallas, Texas, commandeered a Toronto-bound Air Canada jet and ordered the pilot to Cuba. Beasely never made it: he gave himself up at Montreal's Dorval Airport and earned six years in prison for his efforts.

The record for round-the-world flight on a commercial airline was set in December 1977 by CP Air passenger agents David Shore and Roger Matheson. The duo completed the round-trip flight from Los Angeles, with stops in Frankfurt, Singapore, and Sydney, Australia, in 63 hours 8 minutes.

BIRDS

Canada's — and the world's — fastest bird is the peregrine falcon, which hits speeds up to 200 miles an hour in pursuit of prey. The second fastest bird is the golden eagle, which reaches 120 mph — but only when chased by a peregrine falcon!

Canada's most monotonous bird is the red-eyed vireo. From dawn to dusk it repeats its infuriating chee-up-chee-up-chee-up . . . as often as 22,000 times daily. Which just may be why it's red-eyed.

The smallest bird in Canada is the calliope hummingbird, which weighs about a tenth of an ounce and is scarcely larger than a bee. Hummingbirds have more feathers per square inch than any other species of bird.

Canada's most northerly birdhouses are on Norman Lockyer Island inside the Arctic Circle — so far north that even Eskimos haven't lived there for centuries. The boxes, stone chambers about a foot high, were built by Vikings about A.D. 1000 to attract eider ducks.

The largest Canadian bird is the rare trumpeter swan. It has a wing span of up to ten feet.

The best place in Canada to view birds is Point Pelee National Park in Ontario. More than 300 species have been sighted there, and some 100 species are regular residents. During the annual bird count, as many as 25,000 birds have been spotted in the park.

And the best place in Canada to see hawks and blue jays is probably Port

Stanley, Ontario. From mid-September to mid-October up to 500 jays a minute can be seen flying south. Between September and January as many as 25,000 hawks wing past daily.

Canada's — and the world's — champion migrant is the arctic tern. It summers in the Arctic and winters in the Antarctic — an annual round trip of 22,000 miles.

The first bird banded in Canada was a robin. James Henry Fleming performed the ceremony in his garden at 267 Rusholme Road in Toronto on September 24, 1905.

Canada's most ridiculous anti-bird measure was taken by the residents of Lakefield, Ontario. A recent bill there prohibits birds from singing for more than a half-hour between 8 a.m. and 10 p.m. From 10 p.m. to 8 a.m. warbling is restricted to 15 minutes.

The world's largest colony of Canada geese, one million strong, nests on Baffin Island's Dewey Soper Migratory Bird Sanctuary; Cape Searle, also on Baffin Island, supports 200,000 northern fulmars, the largest such colony in the world; Marian Lake in the Northwest Territories has North America's northernmost nesting colony of caspian terns; the gannet colony — 35,000 birds in summer — on Quebec's Bonaventure Island is North America's largest; Canada's biggest winter population of waterfowl is found in George Reifel Migratory Bird Sanctuary in British Columbia; Graham Island, one of the Queen Charlotte Islands in B.C., is the world's only breeding ground of the rare ancient murrelet; Canada's biggest colony of double-crested cormorants is at Grand-Pélerin, Quebec; and Last Mountain Lake Bird Sanctuary in Saskatchewan is North America's oldest such preserve.

One of the strangest laws regarding birds is found under Section 331 of the Canadian Criminal Code: the law states that it is illegal to send a telegram or letter *threatening* a bird.

The first all-Canadian chicken was the Chantecler, a mixture of Leghorn, White, Rhode Island Red, Cornish, Wyandotte and White Plymouth Rock chickens. The Chantecler was bred by Trappist monks at Oka, Quebec, from 1908 to 1910.

The world's most prolific egg-laying chicken is Canadian. It's the Starcross 288, a breed developed by Donald Shaver of Galt, Ontario. Aside from laying a record average of 288 eggs a year, the Starcross remains fertile longer than most chickens — 18 months.

The world's worst chicken joke is a law in Dartmouth, Nova Scotia, which makes it an offense "for chickens to cross the road."

BIRTHS & DEATHS

The first white child born in North America was Snorri Thorfinnsson. He was born around A.D. 1005, probably in Newfoundland or Nova Scotia.

Canada is the only country in the world with continuous birth records going back more than three centuries. The registry of births, deaths and marriages began in Quebec in 1621.

The Canadian record for the most descendants is held by Capt. Wilson Kettle of Port aux Basques, Newfoundland. He ranks second worldwide. When he died at 102 he left 11 children, 65 grandchildren, 210 great-grandchildren and 305 great-great-grandchildren — 591 in all.

The first man in Canada to become a great-great-great-grandfather is believed to have been Walter Sitch. He became eligible on April 28, 1968, when his great-great-granddaughter gave birth to a son in Halifax. Mr. Sitch was 98 at the time of the birth.

The longest-lived Canadian was probably Pierre Joubert. He died in 1814, aged 113 years 124 days.

Newfoundland's Mrs. Ellen Carroll was supposedly more than 115 years old when she gave up the ghost in 1943, but reliable records of her birth date are not available.

Canada's oddest baby boom occurred in 1927 when lawyer Charles Millar died and willed his fortune to the Toronto mother who could give birth to the most children in the ten years following his death. The race to the maternity ward — the newspapers called it the Stork Derby — ended on May 30, 1938, when four mothers divvied up Millar's $568,000 estate. But they didn't have much left to spend on themselves: each had produced nine children.

The first quintuplets in medical history to survive were the Dionne children: Annette, Cécile, Emilie, Marie and Yvonne. (The odds against such a birth are 57 million to 1.) The famous five were born on May 28, 1934, and until they were about seven they were heralded as the number-one peep show in North America. Some five million tourists came to gape at them from behind one-way mirrors; and fast-food stands, souvenir shops, bus lines and gas stations sprang up around their parents' tiny farm near Callander, Ontario. Mother and father hardly saw their children, for the quints were sequestered in a specially built nursery on the farm. Endorsements and movie offers flooded in. The Canadian government set up a $1-million trust fund for the babies. But until they turned seven they were wards of the state under the care of Dr. Allan Dafoe, the man who had delivered them.

Today Marie and Emilie are dead. Yvonne, Cécile and Annette live on the outskirts of Montreal.

Canada's most unusual birthday may belong to Mr. Ten Piling of Cardston, Alberta. Why Ten? He was born on the tenth hour of the tenth day of the tenth month. What's more, he was the Piling family's tenth child. And at birth he weighed — you guessed it — ten pounds.

We've found a place where some Americans are really Canadians . . . sort of. That's at Calais, Maine, right across the border from St. Stephen, New Brunswick. For years Calais' hospital lacked a maternity ward, so expectant mothers were sent to St. Stephen's Charlotte County Hospital. Infants received a Canadian birth certificate, but on returning to American soil they became U.S. citizens by prior agreement. Calais' hospital now has birthing facilities but a few U.S. mothers still have their babies in St. Stephen. And the communities go right on answering each other's fire alarms, worshiping at each other's churches and attending each other's bake sales.

The cheapest funerals in Canada are in British Columbia. Recent figures peg the cost of a standard funeral there at $650. Quebec is the most expensive place to die: the average burial there costs about $1,500.

One of the most expensive Canadian funerals on record took place in the 1850s when John "Cariboo" Cameron's wife Sophie passed on. Cameron, a British Columbia prospector who had struck it rich during the Barkerville gold rush, offered $12 a day and a $2,000 bonus to anyone who would help carry his wife's body to the West Coast. Seven people volunteered. They pickled old Sophie in alcohol, placed her in a 450-pound lead-lined box, and put the box on a toboggan along with a barrel of rum and a bag of gold dust. Then they slid their cargo through 50-below-zero weather to New Westminster, 300 miles away. Sophie was shipped from there to her final resting place in Ontario.

After the funeral Cameron returned to the Cariboo country. Eccentric as ever, he purchased his own private cemetery, and was buried there in 1858.

The only existing ticket to Napoleon's funeral, which took place in 1821, is owned by Canadian Stanley Schwartz. It's part of the largest collection of Napoleonic relics in Canada.

Canada's first college course for undertakers was initiated at Ontario's Humber College of Applied Arts and Technology. First year consists of courses in embalming, anatomy, morals and ethics, and restorative work. Second year is spent in funeral parlors.
   We trust that students learn such underground slang as "rowboat," Canadian funeralese for the cheapest coffin model.

The first Canadian funeral home for animals was Starlite Pet Coffin Reg'd. The Montreal firm specialized in custom-made coffins. Aside from cats and dogs, it laid to rest such animal oddities as a raccoon named Cleo, a Peruvian pig called Angus and a 1,000-pound horse. Other customers included an iguana, a llama, a monkey, a leopard and — yes — a goldfish.

The tombstone closest to the Canada-U.S. border is at St. Basile, New Brunswick. It's only 25 yards from U.S. soil and marks the resting place of Remi Gauvin, who died on June 8, 1960.

The oldest grave in Canada — and probably the world — is at L'Anse-Amour in Labrador. The circular cobblestone mound dates from about 7,000 years ago.

Canada's longest-preserved body is probably that of Derrick Van Laan, a whaler who died in 1740. He was entombed along with identification on the shore of Frobisher Bay. Discovered by an expedition in 1902, the body was perfectly preserved. The tomb was resealed and the body, presumably, is still refrigerated.

BOOZE

One of the biggest binges in Canadian history took place at Port Rowan, Ontario, in November 1922, at the height of prohibition. That's when the steamship *City of Dresden* foundered and spilled her entire cargo — some 6,000 gallons of bottled whiskey bound for Mexico — into the waters of Lake Erie. The residents of Port Rowan scoured the beaches and hid their illicit gains under floorboards and in eaves troughs, swamps, cisterns and compost heaps. One farmer sowed his fields with whiskey bottles; another cached the elixir in a pigsty. And they drank . . . and drank . . . and drank. Most of the whiskey has long since been guzzled, but an occasional bottle still surfaces. At almost six decades and counting, it must be mighty tasty.

The driest town in Canada is Rae-Edzo in the Northwest Territories. If you're a drinker, steer clear — the only bars you're likely to see are the ones in the local jail. An ordinance there prohibits drinking, and anyone caught talking to a lamppost is liable for a $500 fine or 30 days in the clink. Bootleggers face a fine of $1,000, four months in jail, or both.

Canada's first native hooch was spruce beer, drunk by Samuel de Champlain and friends in the early 1600s. The expression "all spruced up" is thought to have referred to the effects of this liquor.

The oldest wine company in Canada is Barnes Wines, founded in 1873 at St. Catharines, Ontario. Barnes is the only Canadian wine that can be bought in every province.

Canadians drink about 29 million gallons of wine each year. If that were served at a single communion, the length of the communion rail would have to be more than 250 times the width of Canada.

The largest winery in Canada is Bright's, established in 1874. It bottles about 4½ million gallons of wine each year — enough to fill 22 Olympic-sized swimming pools.

Canada's oldest drinking house is the Auberge Le Vieux Saint-Gabriel in Montreal. The building dates from 1688, the inn itself opened in 1754, and its first liquor permit was granted in 1769

The world's largest distillery is Seagram's Ltd. of Canada, which makes Seagram's V.O., the biggest-selling Canadian whiskey in the world. In 1977 Seagram's grossed more than $2 billion. Part of that revenue was from outside holdings, but if it were all derived from alcohol sales it would be equivalent to about 3,140,000 gallons of whiskey and wine, or 140 gallons per Canadian.

Canada's first tavern was opened by Jacques Boisdon in Quebec on September 19, 1648. Women, however, weren't allowed into such establishments until the early 1970s. One of the first brasseries to admit females was Le Manoir in Pointe Claire, Quebec. Shortly after it opened to the fair sex, business increased 100 percent.

The city with the most bars in Canada is Montreal. There are more than 2,000 establishments licensed to serve liquor in the city.

The best place in Canada to be imprisoned — if you're a bankrupt drunk — is British Columbia. A law there requires jailers to bring convicted debtors a pint of beer on demand.

Among the most colorful Canadian expressions for liquor were those coined by smugglers and cowboys out west. Their nicknames for booze included bug-juice, tangle-foot, pizen, coffin-varnish, and blue-joint. Whiskey smugglers were called keg angels.

Canada's canniest collector is Horst Wendland of Dollard-des-Ormeaux, Quebec, who owns the largest collection of beer cans in Canada. At last count he had 3,360 *different* beer cans. His prize is the world's first beer can, the Kreuger Flat Top, turned out on January 24, 1935.

The heartiest beer drinkers in Canada live in the Yukon. Despite a hefty price of more than $12 for a case of 24, the Yukon's average annual per capita beer consumption is about 28 gallons.

Canadians rank twelfth among the world's beer drinkers, averaging almost 18 gallons per person annually. The total consumption is almost 423 million gallons — or enough to keep Toronto crocked for three months straight.

The Canadian record for campus beer-drinking is held by students at Ottawa's Carleton University. In a single year they imbibed a staggering 1.3 million pints of beer (cost: $700,000), averaging 304 pints per person. The national average is a mere 144 pints.

One of Canada's most unusual methods for weeding out drunks is the "Freddy Fudpucker," a cocktail served in a bar in Flin Flon, Manitoba. It consists of equal parts of vodka, tequila, Galliano and orange juice. The catch? As soon as you can't say Freddy Fudpucker, you're cut off.

Canada's most expensive drink? That's probably how François Courchesne regards the one he had at the Quebec City Hilton in August 1977. While the Montreal jeweller was sitting at the hotel bar, a case of rings was stolen from his car. But the biggest blow came when his insurance claim was disqualified by Lloyd's of London. Total cost of Courchesne's drink: $38,000.

BOY SCOUTS

The world's oldest active boy scout is Mr. Walter Wood of Kentville, Nova Scotia. And how's this for devotion: in 1976 he spent his hundredth birthday polishing apples for boy scout Apple Day.

The world's speed record for tying the six *Boy Scout Handbook* knots belongs to Calgary's Ken Purnell. He wrapped up clove hitch, sheet bend, sheepshank, bowline, square knot, and round turn and two half-hitches . . . all in 10.9 seconds.

BUGS

Canada's largest collection of worms belongs to Carl Klauck of Holland Landing, Ontario. He has more than 10 million Alabama red wigglers — which is pretty good considering he started with only 3,000. Actually Klauck is an inventor: he uses the little critters to purify soil. And what do they eat? About 75 tons of garbage a week.

The loudest insect in Canada — and the world — is the male cicada. Its call can be heard up to a quarter of a mile away.

Canada's fastest butterfly is the ubiquitous Great Monarch — at full tilt it can fly 17 miles an hour.

The rare satyrid butterfly has Canada's most peculiar species range. In even-numbered years it is seen only east of Manitoba's Riding Mountain National Park; in odd-numbered years it is found only west of the park.

BUILDINGS

The tallest freestanding structure in the world is Toronto's CN Tower, at 1,821 feet 11 inches. To get near the top you take the world's longest elevator ride (1,450 feet in 70 seconds), or the world's longest staircase (2,570 steps: about 20 minutes coming down, a lifetime going up). The 130,000-ton tower is also the world's highest lightning conductor: it gets struck as often as 200 times a year. When construction was finished one worker stripped, ran to the stairs and made the longest vertical streak in history. Not to be outdone, three other rooftop workers unzipped their pants and did to Toronto what many Canadians have wanted to do for a long time.

The highest building in Canada is Abbott's Hut, which sits at 9,680 feet on the Continental Divide between Alberta and British Columbia. Built by Swiss guides in 1922, the hut is in Alberta — and its outhouse is in British Columbia.

The world's biggest collection of grain elevators stands at Thunder Bay, Ontario. Combined, the buildings can hold up to 103,900,000 bushels of wheat — or enough to make a loaf of bread for every man, woman and child on earth, with a little left over.

The oldest building in Canada is thought to be Lachine Manor in Lachine, Quebec. It was built around 1670.

Canada's most unusual dwelling is outside Creston, British Columbia. The structure is made entirely of more than 400,000 embalming bottles. It was built by a funeral director.

Canadians have more rooms per home than any other country — an average of almost 5½. This country also has one of the world's lowest densities: only 0.6 persons to a room.

The largest castle in North America is Toronto's Casa Loma, built by wealthy entrepreneur Sir Henry Mill Pellatt in 1911. Designed by Toronto architect E. J.

Lennox, it has 98 rooms, a mahogany-paneled stable, 30 bathrooms, 25 fireplaces, a marble swimming pool, 3 bowling alleys and a kitchen range large enough to roast a whole side of beef.

The largest ballroom in Canada is at Port Stanley, Ontario. It measures 220 by 100 feet.

The oldest tourist information center in Canada is a polka-dot pagoda in Thunder Bay, Ontario. It was built in 1910.

Canada's first public fallout shelter is at Pointe-aux-Trembles, Quebec. Stocked with a 30-day food supply, the two-story concrete structure, 25 feet below ground, accommodates 400 occupants. You can rent a spot in the shelter for about $200 a year. In the event of nuclear war, an automatic telephone system notifies all renters within 40 minutes — which may be 39 minutes too late.

Canada's most haunted house was probably John T. McDonald's property in Baldoon, Ontario. From 1829 to 1831 his home was plagued by bizarre occurrences which were witnessed by countless neighbors. A huge black dog was seen momentarily, then it vanished without a trace. Shovels and pots were mysteriously pitched through the air. A teakettle rose from the fireplace and was dashed against a wall. Food was flung from the Dutch oven. Rocks came tumbling down the chimney and stones were hurled through the windows by unseen forces. McDonald collected the stones, marked them, and tossed them into a nearby creek; days later they again came crashing through his windows. In a single day 50 small fires broke out in the house; as each was extinguished, another flared up. Eventually McDonald's house, the outbuildings and barn burned to the ground — and only then did the strange happenings come to an end.

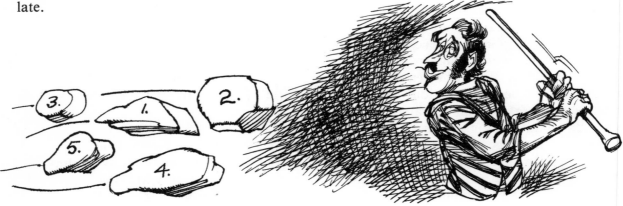

The narrowest house in Canada is 6 Donnacona Street, Quebec. It's only 71 inches wide.

The oldest operating lighthouse in Canada is on Sambro Island, Nova Scotia. Built in 1759 with proceeds from the sale of lottery tickets, it boasts one of Canada's most unusual alarm clocks: a cannon. During the 1800s the gun was fired from the mainland village of Sambro, three miles away, to waken the lighthouse keeper.

Canada's biggest greenhouses are in Brampton, Ontario. They cover an area the size of two dozen football fields. Medicine Hat, Alberta, boasts a single greenhouse that covers about 10½ acres.

What is touted as the world's only U.F.O. launching pad is at St. Paul, Alberta. The pad came unmysteriously into being in 1967 when it was built as a centennial project; it has yet to launch anything.

CITIES & TOWNS

The biggest suburb in Canada may be Mississauga, Ontario. It has over 250,000 inhabitants, more than twice the population of Halifax, Nova Scotia.

The town that would like to be the world's biggest is Biggar, Saskatchewan. A sign on the outskirts reads: NEW YORK IS BIG, BUT THIS TOWN IS BIGGAR.

Canada's lowest-priced town is probably Pacific, British Columbia. Consisting of 11 houses, the remains of a hotel, a ramshackle store and a weather-beaten community hall, the ghost town was purchased in 1976 for a mere $3,200. Doug Aberley was the buyer.

Canada's oldest city is Quebec City. It was founded by Samuel de Champlain in 1608.

The first city in Canada to have more than one million people was Montreal. This happened on October 25, 1951. Pugwash, Nova Scotia, remained unimpressed.

Canada's biggest city is *not* Montreal. Figures for 1977 put Metro Toronto out ahead of Montreal 2,803,101 to 2,802,485 — a difference of only 616 persons.

Canada's largest town at the turn of the 19th century was Port Roseway, Nova Scotia, which was swelled by some 10,000 refugees from the United States. Today Port Roseway is called Shelburne — and its population is only 2,700.

The highest city in Canada is Kimberly, British Columbia. It's 3,661 feet above sea level.

The worst place in Canada to come from — in terms of its name — is Moose Jaw, Saskatchewan. Torontonians, Montrealers, even Haligonians are pretty straightforward names for residents of those cities, but folks from Moose Jaw are called Moosichappishanissippians.

Canada's most photographed village is believed to be Peggy's Cove, Nova Scotia. The cove and its white lighthouse, wharves and small fishing boats attract hundreds of painters and photographers annually. Of course, there are those who say the village was built specifically with that in mind.

The world's most northerly settlement is Alert, in the Northwest Territories. At 81°31′N, 62°05′W, it's closer to Moscow than to Montreal.

COMMUNICATIONS

Canada is one of the three most talkative nations on earth. At last count there were 13,142,235 telephones in this country. If Alexander Graham Bell had earned a nickel for each of the almost 80 billion local calls placed annually in Canada, he would have banked about $4 billion!

Each year Canadians collectively spend the equivalent of 65 years on the phone to overseas countries; we place four million such calls annually, talking for about 8½ minutes at a time. And we make about 850 million long-distance calls *within* Canada each year.

The cradle telephone — similar to the present-day handset — was invented in 1878 by Cyrille Duquet, a Quebec City jeweller. But Thomas Edison was the man who suggested how to use the handset: he encouraged people to answer the telephone with a simple "hello." The phone company had recommended that the user shout "Ahoy! Ahoy!" into the mouthpiece.

Although the telephone was patented in Boston on February 14, 1876, (pat. no. 174,465), it was actually conceived by Alexander Graham Bell in Brantford, Ontario. And it was from Brantford that the world's first long-distance telephone call was made — to Paris, Ontario.

Three nations claim Bell, but the fact is that the Scottish-born inventor emigrated to Brantford in 1870, then moved to Boston and became an American citizen. He spent his last years at Beinn Bhreagh, a magnificent mansion in Baddeck, Nova Scotia. When he was buried there on August 4, 1922, telephone service throughout North America was suspended for one minute at exactly 6:25 p.m.

The first Canadian to lease a telephone — at $42.50 a year — was Prime Minister Alexander Mackenzie.

One of the gravest errors of judgment in Canadian business was made by publishing entrepreneur George Brown of Toronto in the 1870s. He was offered exclusive Canadian and British Empire rights to the telephone — for $150. He turned them down: he didn't think they were worth it.

One of the first two voices on the moon belonged to a Canadian: John Diefenbaker. He and Dwight Eisenhower had their voices relayed in June 1959 during the opening of the Prince Albert Radar Laboratory in Saskatchewan.

The fastest-speaking broadcaster in the world is believed to have been Jerry Wilmot, a Canadian hockey commentator during the early 1950s. His speed: more than 300 words a minute.

The world's first radio station is present-day CFCF in Montreal. It began broadcasting in 1919 as Radio XWA.

Canada's first television station was CBFT, a CBC French outlet, whose first broadcast was on September 6, 1952. Today there are 57 television stations in Canada, and more than one out of every two television-owning Canadians has at least one color TV. Canada's most prolific television viewers are Quebecers. Manitoba watches the least.

The world's first radio broadcast was conducted by a Canadian, Reginald Fessenden, at Plymouth, Massachusetts, on Christmas Eve, 1906.

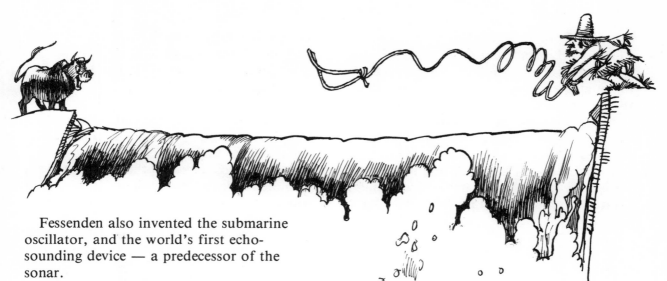

Fessenden also invented the submarine oscillator, and the world's first echo-sounding device — a predecessor of the sonar.

A rather corpulent gentleman, Fessenden once became stuck in the access way of a 400-foot-high transmitting tower. Colleagues failed to dislodge him by pushing and pulling, so they stripped him, lathered him with axle grease and slid him out.

The world's first transatlantic wireless signals were received by Guglielmo Marconi and assistant George Kemp on December 12, 1901. The signal (S in morse code) originated from Cornwall, England, and was picked up at Signal Hill, Newfoundland.

The first announcer to introduce the CBC's 1 p.m. time signal from a hot-air balloon was John Grant. He did so in 1976 while suspended 1,000 feet above Montreal.

COWBOYS & INDIANS

Canada's first black cowboy was John Ware. Nicknamed "The Smoked Irishman," he started ranching in Alberta in the late 1880s. It's no surprise he didn't choose neighboring Saskatchewan: by the early 1900s there were about 40,000 Ku Klux Klanners there.

The world's first Wild West Show was staged at Niagara Falls on August 28, 1872. The center of attraction was to be Wild Bill Hickok, and that's about all the audience — who paid 50 cents apiece — got to see. The crowd wanted Hickok to wrassle and lasso a wild steer, but the star had enough trouble just getting the browsing beast to trot. The buffalo herd, another "highlight," turned out to be a pair of ancient bison who stood motionless and unblinking as attacking "Indians" pelted them with blunt arrows. The spectators were outraged and Sidney Barnett, the show's organizer, was ruined. He headed for South America and became a book salesman. But Buffalo Bill Cody liked Barnett's concept and turned it into a highly profitable venture: Buffalo Bill's Wild West Show.

The world's first stampede was held in Raymond, Alberta, in 1902. The word *stampede* was coined by Mr. Raymond Knight — after whom the town is named.

Canada's most eccentric frontiersman was probably Albertan Jerry Potts, a bandy-legged North West Mounted Police guide and interpreter who trimmed mustaches by firing his six-gun from 25 feet. His uncanny sense of direction prompted some to suggest he had a compass in his stomach, but he was hardly a crack interpreter. He would listen to Indian conversations for hours — and his translation never varied: "He say, he damn glad!"

   Potts might also qualify as one of Canada's biggest lushes: to him a straight line was the shortest distance between two pints. He thrived on whiskey — and when that ran out, he was known to drink red ink.

The world's largest ranch is British Columbia's Gang Ranch. The 2,500,000-acre spread is more than half the size of Prince Edward Island.

One of the greatest oversights in Canadian history was made by the Indians who settled Ontario and Manitoba. For centuries their children played with toys that had wheels — yet never once did the adults think of using wheels for more practical purposes.

Scalping did *not* originate with North American Indians. It was started by Scythians in Russia some 2,700 years ago and first used in Canada by French and British soldiers during the 18th century. Admiring the logic of civilized Europeans, the Indians caught on quickly — a fistful of hair was much easier to manage than a whole head.

The world's biggest tomahawk is at Cut Knife, Saskatchewan. The shaft is 54 feet high and weighs 12,000 pounds; the blade weighs a mere 2,500 pounds. But you should have seen the guy who carried it.

Canada's worst-shod Indians were probably the Chippewas of western Ontario. Chippewa, apparently, is Cree for "people whose moccasins have puckered seams."

Canada's largest teepee is on the Micmac reserve in Maria, Quebec. Made of aluminum, it is 75 feet high and has a diameter of 65 feet at the base. It's used as a church.

Teepees, incidentally, are not the same as wigwams. Teepees are portable, conical dwellings; wigwams are permanent, arched structures.

The world's tallest totem pole was erected at Alert Bay, British Columbia, in June 1973. The 173-foot-high pole tells the story of the Kwakiutl Indians. The world's second tallest totem is the 127-foot 6-inch pole in Victoria's Beacon Hill Park.

Canada's most famous Indian just may be Harry Jay Smith, a Mohawk from Brantford, Ontario. Better known as Jay Silverheels — or Tonto — he rode to fame as the Lone Ranger's trusty sidekick.

The first native-born Canadian to earn a college degree was Louis Vincent Sabatannen, a Huron Indian who graduated in 1781 with a B.A. from New Hampshire's Dartmouth College.

One of the strangest phenomena in Canadian folklore is the ceremony of the shaking tent. The Ojibway Indians employed the ritual to summon the Great Turtle, a tribal god. As night fell they gathered around a massive wigwam covered with moose skins. With the appearance of the medicine man, the tent shook violently and twinkling lights danced about its top. Eerie voices, sobs, screams and the sounds of howling wolves and baying dogs came down from the sky in a sudden blast of wind.

For more than 300 years white men, among them explorer Samuel de Champlain in 1609 and artist Paul Kane in 1848, have witnessed this spooky ritual. Some have called it a fraud, but none can explain it.

CRIME & PUNISHMENT

The largest judicial circuit in the world is in the Northwest Territories. It covers some 1,304,900 square miles and is inhabited by a mere handful of people: about 12,000 whites, 11,000 Inuit and 6,000 Indians.

The first detachment of North West Mounted Police was formed on August 31, 1873. Yet despite the Mounties' reputation as the world's finest police force, early recruits were hardly that: one had syphilis, two could see out of only one eye, and several others had scurvy.

Although the Mounties are famed for always getting their man, they actually lost their first prisoner. William Bond, a whiskey trader arrested at Pine Coulee, Alberta, in 1873, escaped to the United States — and was never recaptured.

The first woman to join the RCMP was Toronto's Heather Ann Phyllis. She quit in September 1976 — to get married.

The Plains of Abraham were named after Abraham Martin, a local shepherd. But we wonder why: On February 15, 1649, the same Mr. Martin was arrested for fooling around with a young girl. He was charged with indecent exposure.

Canada's lowest urban crime rate is in Kitchener, Ontario: it has only about 15 incidents per 100,000 persons. Vancouver, on the other hand, has the highest rate in Canada: 175 per 100,000.

The dumbest robbers in Canada must be those who held up a Ste-Agathe, Quebec, bank in 1974. Police, who were without a lead in the $95,000 theft, studied films taken during the hold-up and recognized one of the culprits as a local resident. The bandit had raised his hood to comb his hair!

Canada's most incredible con artist was Edward Arthur Wilson, alias "Brother Twelve." He bilked a fortune in cash and valuables from dozens of wealthy women, including $65,000 from a 65-year-old dowager. Wilson established the Aquarian Foundation, a cult embracing free love, black magic, voodoo and occult astrology.

The artful trickster, who often wore a ruby-studded hat, mesmerized his followers with hypnotic eyes and a mellifluous voice. He ruled from "The House of Mystery," a magnificent island home off Nanaimo, British Columbia, ringed with gun nests and stocked with rifles. He enslaved his devotees, spent their money, took women to his bed. He forced some to harvest strawberries from dawn to midnight for his favorite jam. He threatened rebellious Aquarians with curses, banished them from his island empire — or murdered them.

Finally brought to trial, Wilson simply cast a spell on the court; judge and jury took sick and doctors were called in. When court resumed, the prosecution's chief witness had disappeared, and Wilson was acquitted. But in 1932 Wilson's followers, tired of their mistreatment, went to the police. They returned with the law to find the island's buildings in a shambles, machinery destroyed, trees uprooted and "Brother Twelve" gone. With him went gold bricks, almost $400,000 of his faithfuls' cash — and 10,000 jars of strawberry jam.

The oldest surviving official Canadian document is a pardon of Aussillon de Sauveterre, accused of killing a sailor. It was signed by Pierre de Roberval on September 19, 1542.

Canada's first unsolved murder occurred in 1633. Etienne Brûlé, one of the continent's earliest explorers (and the first white man to negotiate Quebec's Lachine Rapids), was the unlucky victim. After 12 years among the Hurons, enjoying the amorous attentions of nubile Indian maidens, Brûlé disappeared. Historians speculate that he was roasted and eaten; but the proof, presumably, was in the pudding.

The last public military execution in Canada took place at Fort Battleford, Saskatchewan. In 1885 eight Cree Indians were hanged for their part in the North West Rebellion.

The last public civil execution in Canada was in Goderich, Ontario, on December 7, 1869. Nicholas Mellady Jr. was hanged for murdering his father.

Canada's second last public civil execution took place in 1868 when Patrick James Whelan got the rope. He had shot D'Arcy McGee — in Canada's first political assassination.

And the last judicial hanging in Canada took place at Don Jail, Toronto, on December 11, 1962. Ronald Turpin and Arthur Lucas were executed for murder.

Canada's first hanging under British rule took place in Kingston, Ontario, in 1788. The culprit was executed for stealing a watch — and later declared innocent.

The biggest cash heist in North American history occurred in Montreal in July 1976. Brinks will never forget it: the thieves helped themselves to a cool $2,800,000.

Canada's last fatal duel took place in 1833 when John Wilson killed 20-year-old Robert Lyon. Lyon had insulted Wilson's fiancée; in court, Wilson contended that he was forced to kill Lyon to save face. He was acquitted and later became a judge in the Ontario Supreme Court.

The longest kidnapping for ransom in Canadian history occurred when Charles Marion, a 57-year-old credit union employee, was abducted from his summer cottage near Sherbrooke, Quebec. The kidnappers demanded $1 million for his release, but eventually settled for $50,000. Marion's 82-day ordeal ended on October 28, 1977.

FAIRS & CIRCUSES

Canada's first circus took place in Quebec in 1798. Most early circuses were actually traveling zoos, featuring bears, eagles, foxes and other Canadian wild animals. A Toronto circus in 1827, however, *did* feature a juggler — the circus owner's wife.

The fastest end to a Canadian circus came in September 1827. While 8,000 spectators watched and carnival music filled the air, bankrupt owners of the unsuccessful enterprise loaded bears, bison and chimps two-by-two aboard a schooner — and sent them over Niagara Falls.

The world's first Kiddieland was created by J. W. "Patty" Conklin, a Winnipeg impresario who in 1929 founded Conklin Shows Ltd., now the largest midway concessionaire in the world.

The world's longest roller coaster is the 4,800-foot "Comet" in the Fort Erie, Ontario, Crystal Beach Park.

The record for the greatest number of consecutive rides on the Pacific National Exhibition's roller coaster is held by Laing Smith of Vancouver. Laing made 201 trips in 10 hours. The feat cost him $60 in tickets, but he eventually got to ride free — he became brakeman on the coaster.

The Quebec Winter Carnival is the largest winter carnival in the world, and the third largest of any kind after Rio de Janeiro's carnival and New Orleans' Mardi Gras. The annual bash in Quebec costs taxpayers some $1.5 million.

The largest annual fair in North America is Toronto's Canadian National Exhibition, founded in 1878. The CNE also boasts the world's biggest portable stage: 9,600 square feet.

FASHION

One of the first mirrors in Canada was owned by Hélène de Champlain, wife of the famous explorer. She brought the mirror from France in 1620 and wore it around her neck like a pendant. Local Indians idolized her, for as each saw his image reflected in the mirror, he believed it was *his* picture she carried close to her heart.

We're not sure what this means, but it must signify something: Women in Vancouver spend an average of $2.50 out of every $100 spent on clothes on panties; women in St. John's, Newfoundland, on the other hand, spend only $1.40.

Canada's most bizarre clothing ordinance is the one in Toronto which prohibits patrons of public steam baths from wearing felt hats.

The slouch hat, popular with such screen luminaries as Humphrey Bogart, Edward G. Robinson and George Raft, and a symbol of gangsterism in the 1930s, was originated by Toronto-born Sammy Taft.

The oldest sunglasses in Canada are in the Kings County Museum at Hampton, New Brunswick. They date from 1790 — and they're adjustable.

Recent statistics show that Canadian women use an average of 2½ pounds of cosmetics a year. New York women evidently have more to hide: they use 9 pounds a year.

FILM & THEATER

North America's first play was staged by poet and soldier Marc Lescarbot in 1606 at Port Royal, Nova Scotia. Set against the natural backdrop of Acadian hills and the sea, the play, whose central character was King Neptune, used Micmac braves and French troops as actors. Halifax's Neptune Theatre was so named to commemorate the event.

The first play written and produced in Canada was *Acadius, or Love in a Calm*, a three-act comedy penned in Halifax in 1774.

Our choice for the most original title of a Canadian literary work is that of Wilfred Watson's play: *Oh Holy Ghost DIP YOUR FINGER IN THE BLOOD OF CANADA and write, I LOVE YOU.*

The first Canadian feature film was *Evangeline*, a dramatization of Henry Longfellow's poem of the same name. It was made in 1914.

Canada's first talkie was *The Vikings*, shot in 1930. Its subject: the Newfoundland sealing industry.

North America's oldest continuing film festival is the Yorkton International Film Festival, held in alternate years at Yorkton, Saskatchewan — a town of only 14,000.

Canada's first permanent cinema is believed to have been the Edison Electric Theatre, opened in Vancouver by John A. Schulberg in 1902.

Montreal's Ouimetoscope was, according to its founder Ernest Ouimet, the world's first deluxe movie house. He was probably right: opened in 1907, the 1,000-seat theater featured such novel embellishments as upholstered seats, a six-piece orchestra, a checkroom, seating reservations and an intermission.

Canada's first drive-in movie theater opened in Hamilton, Ontario, on July 10, 1946.

FIRES & EXPLOSIONS

Canada's largest known forest fire raged through the Miramichi River valley in New Brunswick in 1825. The blaze devastated more than 2,000 square miles of forest and claimed 160 lives.

About 800,000 acres of prime Canadian forest are consumed by fire annually; and fire breaks out in a Canadian home every ten minutes.

What may be Canada's longest-burning fire is at Fort Norman in the Northwest Territories. A bed of low-grade coal has been smoldering there since before 1789.

The longest-burning lamp in Canada is at the Ursuline Convent in Quebec City: its flame was lit in 1717 and has never been extinguished.

The first time the Olympic flame ever went out during a Games was at Montreal in 1976. In typical *Québec sait faire* spirit, the torch was rekindled with a rolled-up newspaper.

Government bureaucrats now have more paperwork to play with: the Bomb Threat Procedures Form. In the event of a telephoned bomb threat, public servants are instructed to ask immediately where the bomb is, why it was put there, what it looks like and where the caller is phoning from.

Oh — and the caller's name, please.

The form apparently originated after a female employee received a package that emitted an ominous ticking. When the bomb squad arrived, they quickly got to the root of the problem: the package contained a battery-operated phallus-shaped vibrator.

The world's largest accidental non-nuclear explosion occurred in Canada on December 6, 1917, when two ships, one carrying munitions, collided in Halifax harbor. The explosion killed almost 2,000 persons and injured 800.

For ferry operator G. A. Holmes it was a rather unsettling experience. He was hurled two miles by the blast and landed in an ash heap, naked except for his rubber boots. But the biggest shock came to Mrs. Jean Finigan, a 22-year-old paralytic who had been bedridden for years. After the explosion she was able to walk again.

The world's largest non-nuclear, non-accidental explosion took place in 1958 when Ripple Rock, off the coast of British Columbia, was blasted out of existence. The rock, barely submerged in a navigation channel, had caused dozens of shipwrecks. Some 370,000 tons of stone were shattered in the detonation.

The oldest fire fighting vehicle in Canada is in Shelburne, Nova Scotia. Presented to the town by King George III, the wooden wagon has fixed front wheels (it had to be dragged around corners) and a leather hose. It dates from 1786.

Canada's largest collection of fire engines is in the Fire Fighter's Museum in Yarmouth, Nova Scotia. The collection comprises 34 vehicles; the oldest dates from 1819.

Killarney, Manitoba, claims the world's only *green* fire engine. Its name? The Jolly Green Giant.

In the great fire that destroyed much of the Parliament buildings in 1916, the bell in the center block tower plunged to the ground a split-second before the twelfth stroke of midnight. Ironically, it had been placed in the tower in 1875 as a fire alarm.

FISH

The world's largest creature, commonly found in Canadian waters, is the blue whale. It grows to more than 100 feet in length and weighs up to 150 tons. Even at birth it tips the scales at two tons, then gains nearly 200 pounds a week until maturity. In a single stroke its heart — about the size of a baby grand piano — pumps 2,000 gallons of blood, enough to fill ten king-size waterbeds. Yet strange as it seems, whales and mice develop from the same size eggs.

The largest specimen of the world's largest carnivorous fish, the great white shark, was found in 1930 at White Head Island, New Brunswick. It was 37 feet long.

The biggest squid ever found was a 55-footer, washed up on a beach in Tickle Bay, Newfoundland. It weighed 4,480 pounds and had 35-foot tentacles and eyes 9 inches across.

The world's heftiest crustacean is the North American lobster, plentiful in the Atlantic Provinces. The largest specimen ever found weighed more than 42 pounds.

The biggest lobster pound in the world is at Northern Harbour, New Brunswick. And Conley's lobster plant at St. Andrews, New Brunswick, is the world's largest distributor of live lobsters. Its tanks hold more than 150,000 pounds of the crawling crustaceans.

The only creatures in the world known to have recovered from cancer on their own are Malpeque oysters, a species peculiar to Malpeque Bay on Prince Edward Island.

The longest tuna fish struggle in Canada — and possibly the world — happened near Liverpool, Nova Scotia, in 1934. Six men took more than 3½ days to reel in a 795-pound tuna.

The biggest tuna ever caught was landed at North Lake, Prince Edward Island, by Lee Coffin in 1973. The bluefin, taken with a 130-pound test line, weighed 1,120 pounds. North Lake, not surprisingly, calls itself the "Tuna Capital of the World."

The "Halibut Capital of the World," according to its inhabitants, is Prince Rupert, British Columbia. The average annual catch there is about 160,000 tons — enough to provide fish for every Canadian family for more than a year.

One of Canada's fishiest statements? Investigating the mysterious deaths of 500,000 salmon in British Columbia's Kootenay Lake in 1974, a biologist ruled out pollution as a factor and claimed the fish showed no visible signs of illness. "These fish are perfectly healthy," he told one reporter, "except they're dead."

The biggest lake trout ever caught was a 102-pounder taken from Lake Athabaska in August 1961. Authorities estimated that the fish was at least 80 years old — but they couldn't figure out what sex it was.

The world's second biggest lake trout was caught at Carcross, Yukon Territory, in 1951. It was 5 feet 2 inches long and weighed 87 pounds.

The oldest living fish ever caught was a 215-pound sturgeon pulled out of Lake of the Woods in Ontario. The 6-foot 9-inch specimen is believed to have been 155 years old.

But Lac Pohenagamook in Quebec may contain an even older specimen. For years there have been reports of a black iguana-like creature in the lake. The London *Daily Telegraph* enthusiastically hailed the beast as a cousin of the Loch Ness monster. But biologists think it may be a giant sea sturgeon — which could be more than 155 years old.

Salmon was Canada's first commercially canned food. It was initially tinned in 1839 by Tristram Halliday near Saint John, New Brunswick.

Campbell River, British Columbia, claims to be the salmon-fishing capital of the world.

The biggest sardine- and herring-canning factory in the British Commonwealth is at Black's Harbour, New Brunswick.

Canada's oldest fish company — and the second oldest existing company after the Hudson's Bay Company — is Zwicker & Co. of Lunenberg, Nova Scotia. It was founded in the 1780s.

FOOD

The world's largest hot dog was trundled onto the baseball diamond at Montreal's Olympic Stadium in August 1977. Resting on a 40-pound bun, the 9-foot-3-inch-long dog weighed in at 171 pounds 8 ounces — equal to 2,063 standard weiners. The monster was made by Hygrade, which churns out some 100 million hot dogs annually.

The world's biggest hot-dog machine is in the Hygrade Company's Montreal plant. In an eight-hour shift it produces 576,000 hot dogs — or about 55 miles of weiners. If the machine were operated full-time for a year,

it would make enough hot dogs to circle the globe twice. The average Canadian eats about a half-mile of hot dogs in a lifetime.

The oldest breakfast leftovers in Canada were found at Sainte-Marie-Among-the-Hurons, near Midland, Ontario. An eggshell — part of some poor Jesuit's last meal before the Iroquois attacked — is believed to be 320 years old.

If all the eggs consumed annually in Canada were cooked in a large frying pan they would form an omelette big enough to cover St. John's, Newfoundland. The recipe: 472,111,000 dozen eggs and an 11-square-mile frying pan.

Canada's first cheese was made in 1679 — and is still available today. Called Fromage Ile d'Orléans, the pungent round cheese is sold only in Quebec City and on nearby Ile d'Orléans. The secret recipe has been passed down through the Aubertin family since the 17th century.

The first cheese factory in Canada was founded in 1864 at Ingersoll, Ontario. Canda's first cheddar was manufactured there; so was Canada's first big cheese: a 7,300-pound monster made for the New York State Fair in the late 1860s.

But a plant near Drummondville, Quebec, produces more of the world's most popular cheese than any other factory. It churns out more than 33,000 tons of cheddar a year for Kraft Foods.

The world's largest cheese was made in a CPR shed at Perth, Ontario, for display at Chicago's 1893 World's Fair. Weighing 11 tons, the "Canadian Mite" was 6 feet high and 28 feet in circumference — the equivalent of a day's output from 10,000 cows. A person nibbling away a pound a week would take 423 years to eat the whole thing.

To ship the cheese, workers had to remove the wall of the CPR shed and load directly onto two flatbed cars. The cheese was displayed at the World's Fair — until it crashed through the floor of the exhibit building.

The world's premier producer of maple syrup is Quebec. Its more than 10,000 tapped maple trees are a source of about 1.5 million gallons of syrup yearly, or 60 percent of world supply. That's enough syrup to cover eight stacks of pancakes reaching to the moon.

Canada is the world's biggest exporter of honey. Annual production of some 55 million pounds of honey is equivalent to about 2.2 *trillion* bee-loads of nectar. Bees must fly about 50,000 miles to produce a one-pound jar of honey; the average Canadian beehive produces more than 125 pounds of honey each year.

Bovril, the world-famous beverage made from beef extract, was created in the 1890s to keep chilly Montrealers warm at an ice carnival in Dominion Square.

The world's largest free picnic is the CHIN International Picnic, held annually on July 1st weekend at Centre Island in Toronto. The three-day event, which has been held for more than ten years, draws some 160,000 people. It's free to them, but it costs CHIN Radio at least $200,000 to stage.

Canada's largest birthday cake was the 26-foot-high gateau baked for the British Columbia Centennial in 1971.

The most expensive salads in Canada are found in Ingloolik, Northwest Territories. According to one report the going price is as high as $60 a serving.

The world record for potato eating is held by Robert Service. The poet claimed he kept fit in the Yukon by eating potatoes —

22,000 of 'em annually. Service's boast seems slightly exaggerated: it amounts to 60 potatoes a day!

The first smoked meat sandwich was made in Montreal by Ben Kravitz and his wife Fanny in the 1920s.

No two instant potato flakes are shaped exactly alike — but they were all invented by the same man: E. A. Asselbergs of Canada's Department of Agriculture.

The world's first electrically cooked meal was served at Ottawa's Windsor Hotel in 1892. It was prepared on a crude grill devised by Thomas Ahearn.

Canadians are among the ten best-fed peoples on earth. Each Canadian annually consumes about 520 pounds of fruits and vegetables — fresh fruit being the biggest commodity — and some 160 pounds of meat. And Canadians positively guzzle milk: altogether about six billion pounds of it, which is roughly 65 times the weight of the *Titanic*. But take heart — West German farm minister Josef Ertl recently reported that the world's best lovers drink lots of milk.

Canada's most expensive milk is in the Northwest Territories. A quart costs up to $2 (beer goes for about half that).

The most famous baby food of all was the brainchild of Canadian doctors Drake, Brown and Tisdall. They concocted the formula for Pablum — a Greek word for food — in the 1930s.

Canada's first earthworm recipe contest was held in 1977 by George Main, owner of the Livewire Bait Farm in Richer, Manitoba. To prepare worms, Main advises, store them in peat for 24 hours, then boil them three times in lemon and water and bake at 350° F (177° C) for about 10 minutes. Entries to his contest included worm soup, worm-stuffed cabbage rolls and worms à la hollandaise. We might add our own tried and true favorites: worm potpie, worm quiche, sweet and sour worms, and worm-burgers.

Canada's biggest eaters were probably the 8,000 Olympic athletes at the Montreal Games in 1976. Feeding them was a truly Olympian task: a staff of more than 1,200 could serve about 10,000 meals in 90 minutes.

The 1,500 tons of food (athletes eat about *8 pounds* of food daily) bought for the Games included: 64,000 loaves of bread and 36,000 rolls; 31,250 dozen eggs; more than 65,000 pounds of sirloin steak; 12,500 pounds of ham steak; about 41,500 pounds of fresh fish; more than 50,000 gallons of ice cream; about 1,250 gallons of olives; 7,500 pounds of coffee; and 96 gallons of maple syrup. And you thought *your* grocery bill was high!

Canadians are among the world's most voracious marshmallow fiends. We eat about 5,000 tons or roughly 743 million of the fluffy white balls each year. Put end to end that's enough marshmallows to stretch the length of the Trans-Canada Highway.

The chocolate bar was invented in St. Stephen, New Brunswick, in 1910, by Arthur Ganong. Today Ganong's Ltd., still going strong, is Canada's only major family-owned candy company. Ganong's firm also invented the lollipop, the chocolate roll, and the Valentine's Heart Box.

Canadians gobble more than 100 million pounds of chocolate annually. But sweet-tooths can take some consolation from Arthur Ganong's regimen. He scoffed three pounds of candy daily for more than 60 years, never put on weight and never missed a day's work because of illness. He died at 83.

The most-chewed piece of gum in Canada belonged to Ricky Mathison of Victoria. In the summer of 1977 he kept the same piece of bubble gum in his mouth for more than three months and established a world record.

The largest Canadian gum manufacturer is the O-Pee-Chee Company of London, Ontario. The firm sells more than 7.5 million pounds of gum annually — enough to blow a bubble twice the size of the earth.

Each year Canadians chew about 20,000 tons of gum. We have clearly forgotten the advice of that doctor who warned in the 1890s that chewing gum would "exhaust the salivary glands and cause the intestines to stick together."

And to wash it all down: the best place in Canada to get a glass of water (if local propaganda is to be believed) is Nanton, Alberta. A nearby spring called "The Tap" provides sparkling cold mineral water which the residents of Nanton tout as "Canada's finest drinking water."

FOOT FEATS

The world's longest recorded journey on roller skates was made in 1967 by Clint Shaw. The 4,900-mile trip from Victoria, British Columbia, to St. John's, Newfoundland, took 225 days.

The Canadian crawling record is held by Gordon Harvey of Verdun, Quebec. In July 1977 he crawled 5⅕ miles in seven hours — but that was almost four miles short of a world record.

The first Canadian to walk from Halifax to Vancouver was John Behan. He made the trip in six months in 1921. The fastest walk across Canada was Clyde McRae's 96-day, 3,764-mile jaunt from Halifax to Vancouver in 1973. He averaged slightly more than 39 miles a day.

A record journey on snowshoes was accomplished by Jean Lagemodière in the winter of 1816. He walked 1,800 miles (some 3.5 million steps) from Winnipeg to Montreal to inform Lord Selkirk that the Red River colony had been attacked.

Lagemodière's wife, incidentally, gave birth to the first legitimate white baby in western Canada; another child, a daughter, was the mother of Louis Riel.

The fastest snowshoer in the world is Quebec's Richard Lemay. In 1973 at Manchester, New Hampshire, he registered an all-time record for the mile: 6 minutes 23.8 seconds. At that speed he could have made it from Winnipeg to Montreal in eight days flat.

The Canadian record for carrying a stretcher with a 140-pound body on it is held by two four-man teams from the Gagetown Canadian Forces Base in New Brunswick. They hauled their load 60 miles in 21 hours.

The first woman to run across Canada was Carallyn Bowes, who arrived at Simon Fraser University in Burnaby, British Columbia, on August 31, 1976, after a 3,841-mile job from Halifax, Nova Scotia. She completed the journey in 133 days, shedding 15 pounds and 13 pairs of shoes along the way.

The Canadian record for nonstop jiving is held by Winnipegger Ken Troy. In 1975 he danced for 42 hours 32 minutes — and wore out dozens of partners in the process.

The world record for getting as low as you can go is held by Marlene Raymond of Toronto. On June 24, 1973, she did the limbo under a flaming bar set only 6⅛ inches above the floor.

The world's top flour-girl is Linda Buck, a logging-camp cook from Moose Lake, Manitoba. In August 1977 she staggered 10 feet with 625 pounds of flour strapped to her forehead and shoulders, breaking her previous record of 600 pounds.

Canada's champion demonstrator is Gabriel Christini, who has picketed outside Quebec's assembly buildings five days a week for more than six years — and is still going strong. The disabled miner is protesting a government ruling that he be compensated only $2.45 per hour for a lung disease.

FURNISHINGS

Canada's oldest bed is in the Ursuline Convent in Quebec City. It dates from 1686.

Canada's only *three*-poster bed was made in Quebec. It dates from about 1885 and is now in Dundurn Castle in Hamilton, Ontario. And if you think that's strange, you should see the two paintings of "Reclining Pigs" that hang nearby.

The oldest pressure cooker in Canada is in the Loyalist House in Saint John, New Brunswick. It dates from 1795.

North America's oldest clock, at the Vieux Séminaire Sulpice in Montreal, dates from 1685.

Canada's largest collection of inkwells belongs to Edith O'Regan of Ottawa. At last count she had more than 150.

Canada's largest collection of salt and pepper shakers is displayed in the Prairie Panorama Museum at Czar, Alberta. Its more than 1,100 cruet sets include shakers in the shapes of trains, ships, oxcarts, covered wagons, bullfrogs, giraffes, ducks, the Eiffel Tower, and an outhouse. And for really spicy meals there's even a shaker in the shape of a bare-breasted bathing beauty — one breast holds salt, the other pepper.

GAMBLING & GAMES

Canada's only legal gambling casino —
replete with can-can girls, ragtime piano
players and Klondike decor — is Diamond-
Tooth Gertie's in Dawson in the Yukon.

Some 8 million Canadians regularly pur-
chase lottery tickets, but the odds of
striking it rich are pretty remote: you have
twice as much chance of being hit by
lightning as you do of hitting the jackpot.

The world record for sinking the most
billiard balls in 24 hours is held by Bruce
Christopher of Belleville, Ontario. He sank
a phenomenal 5,688, or one every 15.9
seconds. Christopher, who earned some $2
million in an eight-year career as a
professional pool hustler, once pocketed
$70,000 for a single game. Lessons from the
champ cost $75 to $500 an hour, and
students have included Paul Newman,
Robert Redford and Muhammed Ali.
Christopher once studied to become a
minister.

The world's only international pool table is
in Dundee, Quebec . . . and Fort
Covington, New York. It's in the Dundee
Line Hotel and you can stand in Canada
and sink the balls in the States. (The lucky
hotelier pays taxes to both communities.)

The first professional pool player to make a
100 break in snooker was Canadian Con
Stanbury. He ran 113 in a Winnipeg pool
hall in 1922.

Canada's marathon yo-yo champs are 20 Ottawa students who yo-yoed nonstop for 24 hours in 1969 — and broke about 500 strings while doing it. One student even took a shower in the process.

The yo-yo was originally devised by natives of the Philippines — as a weapon.

The National Monopoly Championship, one of Canada's lesser-known competitions, attracts more than 5,000 participants annually. Monopoly, incidentally, is easily the world's most popular modern board game. More than 70 million sets have been bought since the game's invention. And the annual issue of Monopoly money vastly exceeds the total annual output of the Canadian treasury.

The North American record for nonstop chess-playing was set by Calgary's Branimar Brebrich. After 17 solid hours of pawn-pushing — playing 20 games at a time — Brebrich completed 214 games (188 wins, 18 draws, 8 losses). Brebrich failed to smash Swedish grand master Gideon Stahlberg's 1940 world record of 400 games — he ran out of opponents.

If John Wilson's card hand wasn't the best in the world, it *was* the tallest. The Port Credit, Ontario, resident's 38-tier tower of 1,240 playing cards had more stories than any house of cards ever constructed.

The world's first table hockey set was created in 1932 by Toronto's Donald Munro. The original model had four-man teams and a steel ball for a puck.

The world pinball wizard is a Sarnia, Ontario, resident. In August 1977 Eamonn Kneeshaw stayed at the flippers for 138 hours straight. He was aiming for 144 — but he fell asleep.

GEOGRAPHY

The Canadian National Atlas, produced in Ottawa in 1905, is thought to be the world's first complete national atlas.

One of the world's most spectacular feats of mapmaking was the charting (at a scale of four inches to the mile) of Canada's 3.8 million square miles. The task, completed in 1967, took 44 years.

The world's largest national park is 17,300-square-mile Wood Buffalo National Park — about 4½ times the size of Cape Breton Island. Straddling the Alberta-Northwest Territories border, the park is a haven for North America's only herd of wood bison, half the world population of rare whooping cranes, and the world's most northerly colony of white pelicans.

The largest provincial park in Canada is Ontario's Polar Bear Park. Lake Erie could fit inside the 9,300-square-mile park with room to spare.

Albertans contend that Lake Louise, in Banff National Park, is Canada's greenest lake. One guide, asked why the lake was so green, quipped, ''The damn tourists keep falling in.''

The world's widest straits are the Davis Straits between Baffin Island and Greenland. They're about 600 miles at the widest.

The highest tides in the world occur near Burncoat Head in Nova Scotia's Minas Basin. In spring they can reach 53 feet.

Canada's largest sand-dune field is on the south shore of Lake Athabasca in Saskatchewan. The 115-square-mile wilderness of drifting sand contains seif dunes up to a mile long and 100 feet high — as big as those in the Sahara desert.

The oldest known Canadian-made globe is owned by the Maclean family of Tatamagouche, Nova Scotia. The pine globe was made in 1820 and is 15 inches across.

Canada's densest lake is 24-square-mile Little Manitou Lake in Saskatchewan. The spring-fed lake is so saturated with salt that a person can float in it to his heart's content. With a specific gravity of 1.11 it's almost as dead as the Dead Sea (1.23).

The world's largest bay is Hudson Bay. It encompasses 7,623 miles of shoreline and an area of 317,500 square miles.

It has been estimated that 75,000 square miles of Canada is under glacial ice. Put differently, even if that ice were only an inch thick, it would still be enough to cool more than four *billion* cocktails.

The world's largest island within a lake is 1,068-square-mile Manitoulin Island in Lake Huron. Manitoulin also contains the largest lake within an island within a lake — 41-square-mile Manitou Lake. Now, Manitou just might contain the largest island within a lake within an island within a lake within . . . .

The largest lake entirely within Canada's boundaries is 12,275-square-mile Great Bear Lake in the Northwest Territories. It's about 5½ times the size of Prince Edward Island.

The world's richest vein of silver was discovered at Cobalt, Ontario, in 1903 when blacksmith Fred La Rose pitched his hammer at a marauding fox. He missed the critter but struck paydirt. La Rose sold his claim for a paltry $30,000 — and in one decade alone it yielded some $300 million worth of silver.

More unfortunate, however, was the case of Alexander MacIntyre, after whom the present-day mine in the Timmins area is named. In 1909 MacIntyre sold his claim for $25 to buy liquor. He spent the rest of his life weeping in his beer: the mine subsequently produced more than $200 million worth of gold.

Cobalt, incidently, has the world's largest display of unprocessed silver, worth about $275,000.

The largest collection of signposts in Canada is at Watson Lake in the Yukon. The town has some 1,500 signs from around the world — most of them brought by tourists. Hammered onto 16-foot poles are such directives as: "Kalamazoo City Limit"; "To Lough, England"; "3,153 miles to Salt Lake, Utah"; and "Knoxville, Tennessee."

Canada's largest island is 195,928-square-mile Baffin Island in the Northwest Territories. It's more than four times the area of Newfoundland. But that may change: Baffin Island is rising six feet every 100 years.

The highest waterfall in Canada is Takkakaw Falls in British Columbia's Yoho National Park. It plummets 1,248 feet — about seven times the height of Niagara Falls — into the Yoho River.

The longest freshwater beach in the world is nine-mile Wasaga Beach on Lake Huron. The beach was the launching site of the first nonstop flight between Canada and Britain.

Canada's highest mountain is 19,525-foot Mount Logan, in the Yukon's St. Elias Range. It would take a 70-ton mole to build a hill that big.

The biggest man-made mountain in Canada is Mount Blackstrap near Saskatoon, Saskatchewan. Built for the 1971 Canada Winter Games, it's a colossal 300 feet high.

The deepest cave in Canada is the 1,720-foot Arctomys Pot on the slopes of British Columbia's Mount Robson.

Canada's largest known crater, the New Quebec Crater near Ungava Bay, was created by a meteor. The crater is 1,325 feet deep and almost seven miles in circumference — big enough to accommodate roughly six trillion Mars bars.

The longest river in Canada is the Mackenzie. It flows 2,635 miles from Great Slave Lake to the Arctic Ocean, draining an area seven times the size of Great Britain.

The biggest landslide in Canadian history occurred in Alberta in 1903 when a massive limestone wedge tore away from the side of Turtle Mountain and hurtled toward the sleeping town of Frank. In less than two minutes some 90 million tons of rocks crashed to the valley floor. When the dust cleared, almost half the town — a mine plant and railway siding, a bank, stores and miners' homes — had disappeared, and 70 people were dead. The debris left by the Frank slide can still be seen today: rocks cover one square mile to an estimated depth of 100 feet.

Canada's most easterly point is Cape Spear, Newfoundland (52°37'W); the most westerly point is Beaver Creek, Yukon (140°52'W); the most northerly is Cape Columbia, Northwest Territories (83°07'N); the most southerly is Middle Island, Ontario (41°41'N). And Canada is almost square; the distance from coast to coast is roughly equal to the distance from the Canada-U.S.A. border to the North Pole — about 3,300 miles.

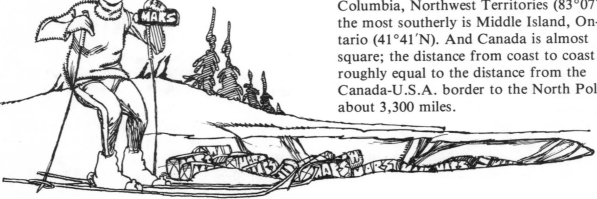

The world's longest undefended border is that which separates Canada and the U.S.A. It stretches 3,989 miles; the border between Alaska and Canada accounts for another 1,540 miles.

The longest place name in Canada belongs to New Brunswick's Lower North Branch Little Southwest Miramichi River. For the shortest, go to A Lake, New Brunswick, or Quebec's Y Lake.

GIANTS

The owner of the biggest feet in Canada was probably Edouard Beaupré. Born at Willow Bunch, Saskatchewan, he weighed 14 pounds at birth, grew to 396 pounds and stood 8 feet 3 inches — so tall, according to one source, that he couldn't ride a horse without his feet scraping along the ground. Those feet took a size 22 shoe.

The Sasquatch, of course, runs a close second. According to measurements the beast's 17½-inch-long feet would require size 21 shoes.

Although his feet were a mere size 14½, Canada's Angus McAskill, who stood 7 feet 9 inches and weighed 425 pounds, had his own claim to greatness. The former "Cape Breton giant" of Barnum and Bailey's Circus smoked probably the largest pipe on record (the size of a carpenter's mallet) and ate some of the biggest breakfasts this side of grizzly country. His morning omelette consisted of two dozen eggs!

McAskill could lift a half-ton on a good day, and legends about his strength are legion. One tells of an American who stopped at McAskill's home at St. Ann's, Nova Scotia. Angus, who was ploughing his fields, was so deep in a furrow that the visitor could scarcely see him as he asked, "Is that where McAskill lives?" Angus shook his head and pointed in the opposite direction — with his plough.

Louis Cyr is reputed to have been the strongest human in history. The 315-pound weight lifter was born in 1863 in Napierville, Quebec. At the peak of his career he could lift 550 pounds with *one finger*; with one hand he could hoist 987 pounds over his head. He once astonished a Montreal crowd by raising on his shoulders a platform loaded with fat men weighing a total of 4,562 pounds. Cyr's hobby? Playing the violin.

Canada's heftiest child was probably Therese Parentean of Rouyn, Quebec. At age nine she tipped the scales at 340 pounds. Her weight at birth is unknown.

The tallest woman born in Canada was Anna Swan. The Nova Scotian Amazon stood 7 feet 11 inches in stocking feet. At birth in 1852 she weighed an astonishing 18 pounds. And for every woman there's a man: Anna married Captain Martin Van Buren Bates, another giant. He was an inch shorter than she.

GOVERNMENT

The highest-paid committee ever appointed by the Canadian government is the Royal Commission on — yes — Financial Accountability in Government. Each of the four commissioners, appointed in 1977, receives $277 a day. That's $70 more than the standard daily fee.

Ottawa's highest-paid public servant is *not* Pierre Trudeau. It's Gerald Bouey, governor of the Bank of Canada. At last cheque, his $75,000 annual salary exceeded Trudeau's by $2,900.

Canada's all-time lowest-paid politician is Regina Mayor Henry Baker. His 1976 salary of $23,400 a year was recently cut — to 8 cents a month.

The most ridiculous government grants ever awarded in Canada? Well . . . in 1972 the federal Local Initiatives Program gave the Dead Men, a Montreal motorcycle gang, $149,477 — to make toys. . . .

. . . and in the early 1970s a government-sponsored project required a group of Stouffville, Ontario, students to stand in a field at 2 a.m. Their mission: "to count the number of birds flying past the moon."

From the *Arab News* in Jidda, Saudi Arabia: "The Canadian government — whose most outstanding feature until now has been the absence of any outstanding feature — has refused to allow the National Chinese to play under their own name."

Canada's best political job description was scribbled in the guest book of Province House in Charlottetown by former prime minister John A. Macdonald. He listed his occupation as "cabinet maker."

Canada's only president was Thomas Spence, an ambitious entrepreneur who tried to establish a republic out of the Prairie provinces in 1867. The capital of Caledonia, as the republic was called, was Portage la Prairie, Manitoba. Spence's scheme bit the dust when he tried to prosecute a cobbler for nonpayment of taxes. He was booted out of town a few days later.

The Canadian Senate, that great pasturing ground in Ottawa, is famous for many forms of inactivity, but this is a record: in 23 years of service, Senator George C. Dessaules never participated in a debate or made a single speech!

The modern-day record for the longest speech in Canadian parliament is held by John Rodriguez of the NDP. In February 1977 he railed against an income tax bill for 6 hours and 10 minutes.

Prime Minister Trudeau was the former record holder: he spoke for three solid hours before his minority government was ousted from office in 1974.

But no one has matched former Prime Minister Wilfrid Laurier's streak of long-windedness. He once yakked for almost 15 hours.

In a singular Canadian ruling Harvey Schroeder, chairman of the British Columbia legislature, recently decided to clean up the language in assembly. Among the words he outlawed: arrogant, chintzy, thick-head, buffoon, and Mr. Magoo.

One of the most sexist Canadian government ruling was passed on October 18, 1929, when the Privy Council officially conceded that women were "persons."

Canada's largest flag was stitched in 1977 for the federal government by Kennedy's Specialties Manufacturing of Erin, Ontario. As many as ten seamstresses worked on the 50-by-25-foot banner.

The only prime minister of Great Britain born outside the United Kingdom was Canadian Andrew Bonar Law, elected in 1922. The only prime minister of Canada born in Great Britain was Sir Mackenzie Bowell, elected in 1894.

A quirk of fate might have had us watching migrating Mesopelagia geese, tuning in to the Mesopelagia Broadcasting Corporation, and singing *O Mesopelagia*. Mesopelagia was just one of the names the Fathers of Confederation considered before deciding on Canada. Other suggestions were: Cabotia, Laurentia, Boretta, and — God forbid — Ursalia.

The name we finally ended up with is generally thought to originate from the Iroquois *kanata* or *kanada*, meaning "village" or "community." The word first appeared in Jacques Cartier's records of his second voyage to Canada in 1535.

We prefer the *Kingston Gazette*'s 1811 explanation of Canada's origin. It whimsically suggested that the word derived from early settlers who spoke of drinking a "can a day" of spruce beer.

Canada's seventh parliament, from 1891 to 1896, was led by a record number of prime ministers — five in all, only one of whom was elected by popular vote. Two died in office: John A. Macdonald in June 1881 and John Thompson in December 1894; John Abbott resigned because of poor health in 1892; Mackenzie Bowell threw in the towel when his entire cabinet quit in April 1896; and Charles Tupper lost the 1896 election to Wilfrid Laurier.

Canada's most frivolous political group is the Anarchist Party of Canada, who define themselves as Groucho-Marxists. One of their most memorable motions: throwing a cream pie in the face of Eldridge Cleaver, famed political activist of the 1960s.

If brochures are any indication of intelligence, then employees of the Department of Transport certainly have a problem. A recently issued booklet, *At Home With Transport*, lists the following rules of office decorum:
• "Do not stand, walk or crawl on the air-conditioners."
• "Leave your pencil at your desk when going to the washroom. Walls are for privacy, not poetry."
• "Liquids or other wastes . . . should not be deposited in plant pots."
• "Face the front of the elevator or you might miss your floor. Pick the elevator that has the light on. The ones without lights might leave you waiting."
• And of course, as every elevator user should know: "Don't remove your hat."

Newfoundland became a province of Canada on April 1, 1949. But the event is celebrated at the end of March — to avoid April Fool's Day.

The best way to live outside the law in Canada is to become a diplomat. According to a recent report, foreign diplomats in this country escaped prosecution 5,516 times in a 12-month period. The charges, dropped because of political immunity, ranged from traffic violations to shoplifting and theft. Uganda recently topped the list for traffic offenses: Idi Amin's five registered diplomats were involved in 611 violations in a 12-month period.

The youngest eligible voter in Canadian history was *so* young she had difficulty mastering the crucial X she would need on election day. Andrea Sparrey, whose name accidentally appeared on a 1976 Toronto municipal voters' list, was eleven . . . months, that is.

Winnipeg's first civic election occurred on January 5, 1874, when 304 registered voters headed for the polls. There was only one hitch: 331 ballots were cast.

The first native representative of the Northwest Territories Council was elected on October 18, 1965. His name? Abraham Allen Okpik.

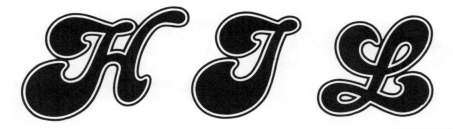

HIGHWAYS & BYWAYS

The world's longest street is Yonge Street, which starts at Toronto's lakeshore and runs roughly 1,170 miles (it becomes Highway 11 after it leaves the metropolitan area) to Rainy River on the Manitoba-Minnesota border.

When Yonge Street was a dirt track, travelers often became stranded up to their waists in mud. It is said that one, when pulled from the mire, cried: "Ah, but wait till I take me feet from the stirrups!"

The longest cantilever bridge in the world is the 3,239-foot Pont de Québec. It spans the St. Lawrence River and carries two roads and a railway line.

The world's longest covered bridge is the 1,282-foot structure that spans the St. John River at Hartland, New Brunswick.

And the 3,334-foot bridge over Quebec's Cap Rouge River is the longest railway trestle bridge in North America.

The world's shortest international bridge is only 50 feet long. It links two of the Thousand Islands in the St. Lawrence River. Half of the bridge belongs to Canada.

The oldest cart tracks in Canada are on Melville Island in the Northwest Territories. The ruts, left by Sir Edward Parry's arctic expedition of 1820, are clearly visible; vegetation grows so slowly in the far north that nothing — not even moss — has obscured them.

Canada's first streetlamps were installed in Montreal on November 23, 1815. They were fueled not by gas or electricity, but by whale oil.

The narrowest street in Canada is Sous-le-Cap, in Quebec City. It's about 100 inches wide.

The oldest street in North America is Water Street in St. John's, Newfoundland. It is believed to date from the 1500s.

The longest *indoor* street in North America is the Western Development Museum in Saskatoon, Saskatchewan.

What is touted as the widest main street in Canada is Broadway, in Grand Falls, New Brunswick. It's 125 feet wide.

Canada's longest tunnel is the Connaught Tunnel, which runs through Rogers Pass in British Columbia. It is five miles long.

The highest all-weather pass in Canada is the 5,800-foot Kootenay Skyway in British Columbia.

The longest highway in the world, the Trans-Canada, covers a distance of 4,860 miles. In snail figures that's 295,929,600 inches. Mile 0 of the Trans-Canada is in Beacon Hill Park in Victoria, British Columbia.

INDUSTRY & COMMERCE

Canada's most unusual branch store is in London, England. Woodward Stores Ltd., a department store chain in British Columbia and Alberta, operates an outlet on a 98-foot-long barge docked in the Thames River near the Houses of Parliament.

The world's oldest chain store system is the Hudson's Bay Company, founded in 1670. Now, of course, it's called The Bay.

The largest aluminum smelter in the world is at Arvida, Quebec. It has an annual production of some 450,000 tons. That's enough aluminum foil to wrap 3.5 billion turkeys or 35 billion cheese sandwiches — or Canada, 4½ times.

The world's largest oil can is at Rocanville, Saskatchewan. It stands 28 feet high and is a replica of the locally invented Symons oil can, the most popular oiler ever made.

The world's first commercial oil well was drilled in 1858 in Lambton County, Ontario, by James Williams of Hamilton.
    Canada's first gusher was struck by Hugh Shaw in Petrolia, Ontario, in 1862. It's reported that the well flowed unchecked for a week and submerged the surrounding area under a foot of oil.

Canada's fastest computer sits in the Canadian Meteorological Center in Pointe Claire, Quebec. The Cyber 76 is capable of more than three billion calculations a minute.

Canada's most industrious mathematicians may be the three Newmarket, Ontario, students who in March 1976 constructed a 39-foot slide rule — the longest in the world.

The world's longest crude oil pipeline runs 1,775 miles from Edmonton, Alberta, to Buffalo, New York. It carries 8,280,000 gallons of oil daily — enough to provide four oil changes a year for about 2½ million cars or to keep more than 400 billion pairs of roller skates lubricated for a year.

The father of modern door-to-door selling was Alfred Fuller of Welsford, Nova Scotia. In 1903 he left for New York with $375 in his pocket; two years later he founded the world-famous Fuller Brush Company.

The world's largest operating windmill is on the Magdalen Islands in the Gulf of St. Lawrence. Used as a power generator, it is 120 feet high and 80 feet across. It has been estimated that 100,000 such windmills could produce half the power anticipated from the James Bay hydroelectric project.

The largest atomic energy station in the world is Ontario Hydro's Pickering installation, near Toronto. The reactor generates enough electricity to supply more than a million homes. The only problem is the nuclear waste — by 1985 there could be enough to cover two football fields to a depth of four feet.

The idlest man in Canada is Eddie Baker of Montreal. The self-appointed King of Idleness managed to avoid working for almost 25 years. Except for a stint as a poet, and a cameo appearance in *The Ernie Game* (the part called for him to yawn; it was edited out), Eddie spent most of his life subsisting on a $35-a-week remittance from his family in Massachusetts. His main contribution to society consisted of drinking coffee in restaurants, smoking cheap cigars and sleeping. But inflation even caught up with Eddie: in September 1976 he took a job looking after parked cars.

LITERATURE

Canada's all-time "best seller" wasn't written by Mordecai Richler or Pierre Berton, and it has no sex, no drama, no memorable characters. Yet it had a greater readership than any other Canadian book, newspaper or magazine. At its peak almost 16 million copies — enough to form a stack some 1,500 miles high — were printed annually. Larger editions used more than 1,000 tons of paper and 100 tons of ink. Give up? It was Eaton's catalog, published regularly from 1884 until its demise in May 1976.

The first book printed in Canada, in 1764, was a catechism. The first book copyrighted in this country was *The Canadian Spelling Book*, in 1841.

North America's first novel was written by Frances Brooke. Her four-volume *History of Emily Montague* was published in England in 1769. Brooke, who came to Canada in 1763, was — obviously — North America's first novelist.

The first Canadian novel published in Canada was *St. Ursula's Convent*; *or The Nun of Canada, Containing Scenes from Real Life*. It was written by Catherine Julia Hart when she was sixteen, and published in 1824.

The world's longest poetry reading — 75 hours, 150 poets — was held in February 1976 in honor of the closing of The Bohemian Embassy, a Toronto coffee house. The club, first in Canada to hold regular poetry readings, might have lasted longer if it hadn't been listed in the Yellow Pages under Embassies and Consulates.

B'rer Rabbit, one of the world's favorite children's characters, is based on Canadian Indian legends. The Algonkian Great Rabbit was the prototype.

The only Canadian novel to make it to the top of annual worldwide best-seller lists was *The Silver Chalice*, in 1952. Author Thomas B. Costain was born in Brantford, Ontario.

Some of our best-known clichés came from the pen of Canadian satirist Thomas Chandler Haliburton. The 19th-century author — whose fame equaled that of Charles Dickens — created Sam Slick, the itinerant Yankee clock peddler who uttered such famous homilies as:
- "Six of one and half a dozen of the other"
- "An ounce of prevention is worth a pound of cure"
- "A nod is as good as a wink to a blind horse"
- "Barking up the wrong tree"
- "As quick as a wink"

- "The early bird gets the worm"
- "Raining cats and dogs"
- "Jack of all trades and master of none"
- "Facts are stranger than fiction"
- "Stick-in-the-mud"
- "Upper crust"

Supposedly Haliburton, who was also a Nova Scotia supreme court judge and a member of British Parliament (he moved to England when he was 65) can still be seen today — more than 100 years after his death. Residents of his former home in Windsor, Nova Scotia, have reportedly sighted his specter on several occasions. It emerges from a paneled wall, drifts about, then vanishes through the wall.

The world-famous Hardy Boys were created by a Canadian. The late Leslie McFarlane, who wrote under the pseudonym Franklin W. Dixon, initiated the series in the early 1920s while working as ghost writer for the Edward Stratemeyer Syndicate. He drafted 21 of the Hardy Boys books, and received a paltry $100 for his first manuscript.

Canada's first library was established at Port Royal, Nova Scotia, in 1606 by Marc Lescarbot. The French soldier, lawyer and poet lent his own books.

Canada's largest publishing company is Harlequin Enterprises Ltd. Pumping out 12 titles monthly, the Ontario-based venture chalks up annual sales of more than $80 million. In other words, Harlequin says, if placed end to end the books would stretch twice the length of the Amazon River and equal the weight of 55 Boeing 747 jumbo jets.

Canada's most prolific living writer — and by his own admission the country's "most-read unknown writer" — is novelist Dan Ross, alias W. E. D. Ross, Clarissa Ross, Jane Rossiter, Rose Dana, Dan Roberts, Ruth Dorsett, Ellen Randolph and Tex Steele. Ross, whom the *New York Times* described as "one of the most formidable writing factories in this or any other hemisphere," has published some 115 novels (gothics, westerns, romances, and mysteries) and more than 600 short stories in 22 countries and 13 languages. He once wrote a novel in five days.

William Osler, founder of Baltimore's Johns Hopkins School of Medicine, also deserves mention. The Canadian doctor churned out some 1,200 books and short stories — about 1½ every month of his life.

Uncle Tom, of the famous cabin, was living in Dresden, Ontario, when he was discovered by novelist Harriet Beecher Stowe. Josiah Henson (his real name) was a fugitive slave who came to Canada from Maryland in 1830. Stowe used him as a model for the main character in her novel, *Uncle Tom's Cabin*.

Slavery, incidently, was abolished in Canada in 1793 — more than 60 years before slaves were freed in the United States.

The world's smallest dictionary is owned by Fred Turfus of Montreal. A magnifying glass is a must for reading the 384-page *Bryce's English Dictionary*. It measures only 1 by ¾ of an inch.

Canada's tiniest book printed with movable type is the 28-page *Short Works*, produced by Robert Oliphant of Victoria, British Columbia. It measures $^{11}/_{16}$ by $^{3}/_{8}$ of an inch, about half the size of a postage stamp.

Canada's largest comic-book store is Toronto's Memory Lane Publications, operated by "Captain George" Henderson. Its stock of roughly 20,000 comics includes such gems as Issue No. 1 of *Fantastic Four*, published in 1961 and now worth about $250.

Memory Lane also claims Canada's largest collection of movie posters — about a million.

The world's first comic book, *Funnies on Parade*, was issued in 1933 and featured Joe Palooka, Mutt and Jeff and Hairbreadth Harry. Though not sold directly to the public, it was offered as a gift premium by Canada Dry.

The world's only *living* comic-book character is Canadian. The Human Fly, a Montreal-born stuntman, has taken his place alongside The Hulk and Spiderman as a Marvel comic-book hero.

"The Germans had better start making stronger rope if they want to hold Canadians captive!" With those stirring words Johnny Canuck, Canada's greatest comic-book hero, won the hearts of youngsters across the country in the 1940s. During World War II, when U.S. comics were banned in Canada, readers were entertained by the likes of Dixon of the Mounted, Nelvano of the Northern Lights,

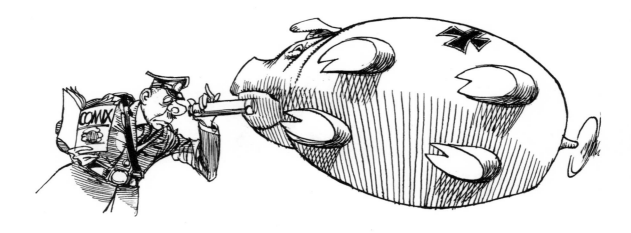

The Penguin, The Brain, and Thunderfist. There was Derek of Bras D'Or, the Canadian superman, who at 15 stood 7 feet 9 inches tall, weighed 500 pounds, and had hands 6 inches wide and a foot long! And let's not forget Ace Barton, who once dispatched 12 armed Nazis with his bare hands. Some comics offered more than just entertainment; Johnny Canuck, for instance, featured this useful information:

"How to recognize a Messerschmitt when it flies over your home."

Superman, the world's most famous comic-book hero, was created by Joe Shuster, a Torontonian. The *Daily Planet* was based on a Toronto newspaper.

The man of steel first appeared in the June 1938 issue of Action Comics.

MAIL

Canada's first post office was established in Halifax, Nova Scotia, in 1755 as a stopover for mail ships sailing between New York and Falmouth, England.

Today there are some 8,500 main post offices in Canada, handling approximately 20 million pieces of mail *daily*.

The world's longest letter was written by Keven Rector of Trenton, Ontario. Starting on January 7, 1974, the intrepid author worked his way through 21½ packages of streamers, 4 pens (2 Bics) and 4 pencils, and emerged — 63,000 words later — with a letter exactly one mile long. (That's not counting the 100-odd feet that his mother accidently sucked into the vacuum cleaner.) The marathon chore, which took 108 hours 10 minutes, ended on May 5th. Darla Legrow, to whom the letter was eventually sent, spent another 14 hours reading the historic document.

The first Canadian postage stamp — the threepenny Beaver — was designed by Sir Sandford Fleming in 1851. (Sir Sandford also originated Standard Time in 1884.)

The longest Canadian postal strike began on October 21, 1975, and lasted 42 days. It cost the post office about $20 million in lost revenue, postal workers some $35 million in lost wages, and Canadian business and industry more than $1 billion in potential sales. But Bell Telephone came out smiling: overseas calls jumped 40 percent during the strike.

One of the longest Canadian postal routes was initiated by Frank Barnard, a Quebecer living in British Columbia during the 1865 Cariboo Gold Rush. He charged $2 to deliver a letter — and walked 500 miles to deliver the first one. But he made so much money that he later started the B-X Cariboo Pony Express — which became the longest stagecoach route in North America.

The world record for recycling a birthday card is held by C. R. Findlay of British Columbia and Douglas Bohn of Seattle, Washington. Since November 1933 they have exchanged the same dog-eared card more than 80 times.

Second place goes to Cyril Halfhide of Victoria, who has received the same birth-day card every July for more than 40 years. Every December 10th Halfhide returns the greeting to Elizabeth Wilson of Brandon, Manitoba, who bought the card in 1936.

Canada's champion Valentine is Meryl Dunsmore of Toronto. Every St. Valen-tine's Day since 1928 she has received a Valentine card from a secret admirer. She suspects the sender is an old beau from her high-school days in Toronto. Whoever he is, the persistent cupid appears to be doing well: a recent card was postmarked Am-sterdam, and the one before that came from Port-au-Prince, Haiti.

MATRIMONY

The second-best reason for getting married in Canada during the 17th century was the king's dowry. Prospective bridegrooms were lured to the altar with the promise of two pigs, two chickens, an ox, a cow, two barrels of salt pork and 11 crowns in coin — and a homely girl thrown in for good measure. The bride's bribe certainly worked: the population of New France jumped from 3,215 in 1667 to more than 8,000 only five years later.

The first Canadian marriage on record took place in September 1654. Today there are more than 200,000 marriages annually in Canada — and more than 50,000 divorces. Albertans have the highest chance of being divorced; Prince Edward Islanders have our sympathy (they have the lowest).

The first homosexual wedding in Canada occurred in 1971 when entertainer Michel Girouard and his pianist, Réjean Tremblay, tied the knot at a Montreal discotheque. The gaiety went out of the marriage four years later, however, when both partners decided to call it quits. There were no children.

The first Canadians to marry on the Citizen Band network were "Buffalo" Bob Kelso and "Rose Petal" Cloughton. They joined wavelengths in late 1976 during a 15-minute ceremony performed by Reverend "Bird Dog" Wyrick.

The first airborne wedding in Canada took place on May 23, 1929, high above Regina. The bride and groom began their marriage on a wing and a prayer — they were passengers aboard a rickety, low-flying biplane.

The largest Valentine ever written in Canada was the 12-by-20-foot billboard erected by Norman Stevenson in Winnipeg. It was addressed to his wife Lore.

Canada's best example of bad timing occurred in 1974. After 20 years of marriage the husband of Mrs. Audrey Robb was divorced from his spouse. A week later she won the $1-million Olympic Lottery.

MEDICINE

The greatest swallowing act in history was that of an unidentified Canadian woman who in 1929 was treated for abdominal pains at an Ontario Hospital. Astounded doctors fished more than 2,500 objects from her stomach, including almost 950 bent pins.

Canada's first doctor was Louis Maheu, born in Quebec on December 12, 1650. In his spare time he was the Quebec City harbor master.

The first woman doctor in Canada was a man — or so thought everyone who worked with her. Dr. James Miranda Stewart was appointed Inspector General of hospitals for Upper and Lower Canada in 1857. For eight years she masqueraded as a male — albeit an effeminate one — until her death in 1865.

The first *orthodox* female doctor in Canada was Emily Howard Stowe. She set up practice on July 16, 1880, in Ontario.

The first Canadian appendix was removed in 1883. The physician in charge was Dr. Abraham Groves.

Canada's first heart transplant was performed by Dr. Pierre Grondin in Montreal on May 31, 1968. His patient, 59-year-old Albert Murphy, died the next day.

The first Eskimo in Canada to wear a wooden leg was an old hunter left crippled after a skirmish with a polar bear. His artificial limb, fashioned in 1830 by a member of Sir John Ross's arctic expedition, was inscribed with the name of the expedition's ship *Victory*.

One of the most common catchwords of the late 1960s originated in Canada. While experimenting with hallucinogenic drugs in Saskatoon, Saskatchewan, doctors Osmond and Hoffer combined the Greek words for "mind" and "expanding." The result: *psychedelic*.

Quebecers are believed to be the world's heaviest tranquilizer users. According to a recent survey, "downers" accounted for almost 38 percent of all prescription drugs consumed in Quebec. Persons enrolled in the province's free drug program filled as many as 80 prescriptions annually. Some had as many as ten complete medical examinations a week.

Canada's first female dentist was Emma Casgrain of Quebec. She graduated from the Quebec College of Dentists and began practising in 1898.

Canada's first successful operation to separate Siamese twins took place in 1971 under the supervision of Dr. Barry Shandling at Toronto's Hospital for Sick Children, Canada's first children's hospital (founded in 1875).
  The world's first Siamese twins, incidentally, were Chang and Eng Bunker, born in Siam in 1811. Not the least of their problems was that Chang was a prodigious drinker, while Eng never touched the stuff.

The world's first mobile clinic was a station wagon, used in 1936 during the Spanish-American War by Dr. Norman Bethune, Canada's most celebrated missionary. While working in China, Bethune was dubbed "Pai-Chu En," which translates roughly as "White man who seeks Grace."

The Canadian Red Cross operates the largest volunteer blood donor system in the world. More than three-quarters of a million Canadians have given blood since the mid-1940s, and some 200,000 Canadians receive free blood transfusions each year. Since 1954 at least 75,000 Canadians have given blood more than 35 times.

MILITARY

The shortest battle in Canadian history occurred on July 17, 1812, when Canadian Captain Charles Roberts and some 600 men marched on Fort Michilimackinac, on an island between Lake Huron and Lake Michigan. The American commander of the garrison surrendered without a moment's hesitation. He hadn't even heard that there was a war on.

The first Canadian to win the Victoria Cross was William Hall, born in 1827 in Avonport, Nova Scotia. He received the award while serving with the British forces in India during the late 1850s.

The only Canadian army officer killed in the Battle of Waterloo was Captain Alexander MacNab.

North America's largest collection of Nazi memorabilia is in the Andy Wright Historical Museum in Swift Current, Saskatchewan. A pearl-handled pistol imprinted with the letters A. H. is believed to be Adolf Hitler's personal handgun — the only one left in the world.

The most half-hearted invasion of Canada took place in 1899 when George Francis Train decided to bridge the Juan de Fuca Strait and lead an army on Vancouver Island — which he intended to give to Ireland. Neither bridge nor army ever materialized, but at 5 a.m. one morning Train went anyway, by boat. He took one look and returned home to Seattle, claiming the island was of little value: the inhabitants just slept in too darn long.

Contrary to popular belief, it was not Snoopy, but a Canadian who shot down the Red Baron. Arthur Roy Brown from Carleton Place, Ontario, clipped the Baron's wings on April 21, 1918.

Canada first entered World War II on September 10, 1939. The song the CBC interrupted to announce the news was "Smoke Gets in Your Eyes." And this was the last song Eva Braun, Hitler's mistress, heard before committing suicide.

One of Canada's most famous heroines is Laura Secord — and almost every Canadian schoolchild knows the story of how she led a cow 12 miles through the darkened countryside to warn the British that the Americans were about to attack. Actually the cow story is a lot of bull — there was no such animal. The man who fabricated the cow incident was N. C. Coffin, a capricious biographer.

Let's applaud the Canadian army for this cogent advice on how to faint: "The fainting soldier should turn his body 45 degrees to the right, squat down and roll to the left, all the while retaining control of his weapon."

The most fought-over pig in Canadian history was owned by a Hudson's Bay Company official on the island of San Juan, near Vancouver. In 1859 it almost started a war. The pig kept straying onto the potato patch of an American neighbor, Layman Culver. After repeatedly warning the pig's owner, Culver shot the porker. In the ensuing quarrel the official claimed the territory belonged to Canada (and thus to Britain); the American contended it belonged to the States. The dispute reached the high courts of both countries — because no one was sure who really owned San Juan. The island was occupied by military from both countries until the dispute was settled 14 years later. Emperor Wilhelm I of Germany was finally called to arbitrate in 1873. He decided in favor of the United States.

The last military engagement on Canadian soil occurred on June 3, 1885, when a North West Mounted Police force led by Major Sam Steele clashed with a band of Cree Indians led by Big Bear. The skirmish took place at Steele Narrows, Saskatchewan, and Big Bear escaped. He was later arrested and jailed.

Steele went on to patrol single-handedly what was probably the largest police beat in history — some 6,800 square miles of the Northwest Territories.

MONEY

The world's most expensive credit card is used by VIPs dining at Toronto's Egan Restaurant. The 24-karat gold discs were made by Sherritt Gordon Mines Ltd. of Fort Saskatchewan.

Canadians are among the world's biggest check-writers. We write more than a billion checks annually worth a total of $800 billion — an amount greater than the cash in circulation in Canada.

Money circulating outside Canada's banks has been estimated at $5,213 million in paper currency and $656 million in coin. Some 200 million one-dollar bills have been produced in Canada: stacked, these would weigh more than 200 tons and reach to the top of the CN Tower four times over. The average life of a Canadian dollar bill is 1½ years.

The hardest place to find two-dollar bills in Canada is the Prairies. People there apparently have an aversion to deuces (old-timers sometimes refer to them as "squaw money" or "devil's money"). That's why the Bank of Canada sends no two-dollar bills to that region; instead it dispatches twice the usual number of ones.

During the Great Depression, when scores of American banks declared bankruptcy, not one Canadian bank went under.

The most expensive windows in Canada are those of the Royal Bank Plaza in Toronto. They're coated with 2,500 ounces of gold worth about $325,000.

The smallest bank chartered in Canada was the Farmer's Bank in Rustico, Prince Edward Island. It was founded in 1864 by Rev. Georges-Antoine Belcourt, the same gentleman who drove the first car in Canada.

Canada's biggest-coin collection — not Canada's biggest collection of coins — is in Numismatic Park in Sudbury, Ontario. The Big Nickel is there: 2 feet thick and 30 feet high. There's also a penny 12 feet high and almost 1½ feet thick.

According to recent calculations, Canada's natural resources — unprocessed — are worth $460 billion and a hundred times that when converted into manufactured products. In other words, if all that money were divided equally, every Canadian would be worth about $2 million — and we could all move to Florida.

North America's first flying bank was a DC-3 that operated out of Yellowknife, Yukon Territory. Owned by the Canadian Imperial Bank of Commerce, it served workers in Port Radium, Coppermine, Lady Franklin Point and Cambridge Bay. It was instituted in the late 1960s.

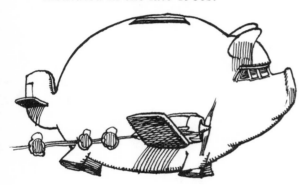

Canada's most valuable coin is a 1911 silver dollar, sold to Douglas Robbins in 1976 for $110,000.

Among the world's rarest coins are those struck in 1862 by James Douglas, then governor of British Columbia. Only a few were made before minters discovered that something was wrong: the $10 gold pieces contained $14 worth of gold.

The best place in Canada to spend a wooden nickel is Gananoque, Ontario. The nickels, generally purchased as souvenirs, are legal tender there.

The miseries of income tax may be as inevitable as death, but they weren't meant to be. When income tax was first introduced in Canada in 1917 it was called "a temporary wartime measure."

MUSIC

An Inuit song making the rounds recently may have the world's longest song title: "EEKALEECAHKATASCHUNEEQKO-VEEAHNAMAREETUYRRALLUAKH." Translated, it means "I love to go fishing in the springtime." The song was penned by Charlie Panigoniak, an Inuit folk singer.

Canada's most prolific unknown songwriter is Toronto's George Cook. Since he wrote his first number, "Under the Western Sky,"

at 13, Cook has penned more than 6,000 songs. But the man who dubs himself the "Gordie Howe of Songwriters" has actually had fewer than 25 songs recorded — and those he taped himself.

Alexander Muir must turn over in his grave every time "The Maple Leaf Forever" is played. Mr. Muir, you see, composed the song to celebrate Confederation. He paid $30 to have 1,000 copies printed, but sold only $4 worth before the song was pirated by a music publisher. The publisher copyrighted and promoted it — and made a bundle.

The largest rock concert ever held in a building in Canada occurred in July 1977 when Pink Floyd played to 80,000 at Montreal's Olympic Stadium. The group brought some $2 million worth of equipment with them. Although liquor was forbidden, one spectator was caught with two gallons of wine, a bottle of gin and three cases of beer.

A record record collection is owned by Ed Moogk of Ottawa. At last count he had some 15,000 discs — all of them Canadian. It's the largest collection of its kind.

The first known Canadian recording was probably one of the dullest platters to hit the turntable: made by Lord Stanley of Preston in 1888, it was called "A Message to the President of the U.S.A."

The world record for nonstop yodeling — 7 hours and 29 minutes — is held by Don Reynolds of Brampton, Ontario. The former Country & Western singer made the grade in November 1976, beating the previous record by more than two hours. Yodeling, incidentally, is a standard pastime among African pygmies.

The winner of first prize in the world's first International Whistle-Off was Canadian lawyer Harvey Pollock. In October 1977 he took top honors in the solo and foreign whistling categories. His prize? A one-foot-high wooden whistle.

Canada's most unusual method of voice control? Well, since Canadian opera singer Maureen Forrester had her first child, she's added 2½ notes to the top of her vocal range and 2½ to the bottom — a note for each of her five children.

Canada's most northerly operetta was written on Melville Island by explorer Edward Parry in 1819-20. It was called, appropriately, "The Northwest Passage." Melville Island at that time was 1,000 miles farther north than the most northerly trading post.

A world record for nonstop organ-playing was set in November 1976 by Steve Katerenchuck of Sault Ste. Marie, Ontario. He pulled out all the stops — for 206 consecutive hours.

NAVIGATION

The first man to sail solo around the world was Joshua Slocum of Westport, Nova Scotia. He circumnavigated the globe between 1895 and 1898, starting when he was 51. Slocum had one handicap: he couldn't swim.

Canada's most famous and best-documented ghost ship is the one Cape Breton Islanders call "The Phantom Ship." It was last seen in November 1929. That night, as with previous sightings, the ship drifted offshore as fire consumed the sails, spars crashed to the deck and the flaming masts toppled into the sea. Then the fiery hull drifted from sight — perhaps never to be seen again.

North America's first steamship was the 85-foot *Accommodation*. It made its maiden voyage on November 1, 1809, between Montreal and Quebec City — and took 36 hours to complete the trip. Its owner was John Molson, the beer baron.

The first steamship to cross the Atlantic was the *Royal William*. Built in Quebec in 1833, it was sold to Spain a few years later. With its name changed to *Isabella Segunda*, it became the world's first steamship from which a gun was fired.

Canada's oldest known message in a bottle was found in Victoria, British Columbia, on December 9, 1936. The message, dated November 19, 1899, was dispatched off the coast of Sweden from the S.S. *Crown Princess Cecelia*.

The longest artificial seaway in the world is the 188-mile St. Lawrence project. It was built at a cost to Canada of about $700 million; the United States chipped in roughly $300 million.

What must be the world's longest journey by canoe began in 1901 when *Telecum*, a 40-foot Siwash Indian dugout, left Victoria, British Columbia. The crew traveled to Australia, India and Africa. Millions of paddle sores later they arrived in England — after a voyage of more than 15,000 miles.

The first North American use of a diver's helmet occurred in 1842 at Pictou, Nova Scotia. The diver was John Fraser, whose brother, J. D. B. Fraser, was the first doctor in Canada to use chloroform.

Canada's first disposable ship was a timber drogher built in 1824. Held together with pegs, it was sailed to England, dismantled, then sold as lumber — all to avoid British timber restrictions.

North America's oldest naval dockyard was begun in 1759 at Halifax, Nova Scotia. It was built by Captain James Cook, the noted explorer of the South Pacific and the Antarctic.

NEWSPAPERS

Canada is the world's largest producer of newspaper, churning out more than 9 million tons annually — or about 40 percent of world supply. That's enough newspaper to wrap a 30,000-square-mile fish, or an area the size of New Brunswick.

The first newspaper in Canada was *The Halifax Gazette*. It was issued on March 23, 1752, by John Bushnell, an unscrupulous entrepreneur who raised funds by marrying a wealthy negress and, 15 years later, a 95-year-old widow. Still, Bushnell never rose to the heights of the founder of Montreal's *Gazette*, which was started in 1778 by Benjamin Franklin — of lightning and independence fame.

Canada's first daily newspaper was *The Montreal Daily Advertiser*, established in 1833. Toronto's *Royal Standard* followed in 1836. By the early 1860s Canada had 249 daily newspapers and 950 weekly or biweekly papers.

Today's Canadian newspapers include 78 *News*, 42 *Stars*, 40 *Times* and 31 *Gazettes*. Some of the more unusual banners: *Lumby Logger, Juan de Fuca News, Age Press, Totem Times, Shilo Stag, Crowsnest Clarion* and — oddest of all — *The Low down to Hull and back News*.

Almost 90 percent of Canadian households receive a daily paper. And 80 percent of the subscribers spend approximately 30 minutes a day reading it.

The world's first accredited female war correspondent was Kathleen Blake Watkins. Better known as "Kit of the Mail," she bagged her first assignment in 1898 — covering the Spanish-American War. Kit was also Canada's first syndicated columnist: for almost 20 years she edited the *Toronto Mail's* "Woman's Kingdom" page, a potpourri of reviews, poetry and advice to the lovesick.

The oldest continuing weekly in the Maritimes is *The Casket*. It was founded in 1842 in Antigonish, Nova Scotia. It's not an underground paper.

Canada's most eccentric newspaper was *The Nor'Wester*, founded in 1859 and the first paper to publish in Manitoba's Red River district. It introduced a little culture — and levity — into the drab lives of settlers and sodbusters with such enlightening articles as "Montreal to be the Residence of the Pope," "The End of the World — 1878 the Last Year," "A Deaf and Dumb Lawyer," "A Three-Tongued Child," "The New Horror: Premature Interment," and "What is the Use of the Moon?"

Foreign news featured such gems as this account: "A man in Albany is troubled with a strange mania. He thinks he is a cancer. Very nearly ate the side of a poor fellow's face off, and then was locked up."

And let's not forget the editor's list of births, marriages and deaths. He called it: "Hatched, Matched and Dispatched."

Canada's most wholesome newspaper was British Columbia's Richman *Review*. In 1970 editor Mickey Carlton published a special edition designed to please everyone and offend nobody. Even mildly off-color material was edited out: there were no crime stories, no angry letters or editorials, no pictures of girls in swimsuits. Even a cow had its udder airbrushed out. The newspaper was not a hit.

PAINTING

The smallest paintings in the world are the work of British Columbia's Gerard Legare. He paints in oils on pinheads only $1/32$ to ¼ inch across.

Canada's most creative house painter is former barber Arthur Villeneuve. He launched his career by painting every wall inside and outside his house in Chicoutimi, Quebec, with landscapes. Today Mr. Villeneuve is one of Canada's most celebrated artists. His first painting sold for $25. Now his work fetches thousands.

The world's most tattoed man was Torontonian Vivian Simmons. When he died in 1965 his body bore 4,831 tattoos, one of which had the enchanting title of "Sinbad the Sailor in the Valley of Rubies."

The world's longest frieze is in the Saskatchewan Museum of Natural History. Almost 460 feet in length, it runs along three walls of the building and displays more than 300 figures of mammals, birds and fish.

PLANTS

The deadliest plant in Canada is the Destroying Angel (*Amanita virosa*), a mushroom so poisonous it shouldn't even be touched. And if you eat it, you have about a 90-percent chance of dying — usually within several hours.

What is believed to be Canada's oldest living tree grows on the southern slope of Waterloo Mountain in Duncan, British Columbia. The Douglas fir was a mere seedling in A.D. 650 — about the time Mohammed founded the Islamic religion and St. Augustine became the first archbishop of Canterbury.

Another Douglas fir, felled and displayed in Duncan, dates from A.D. 636. It could provide enough kindling to fuel more than a million fireplaces.

Canada's most popular Christmas tree is the balsam spruce. One intrepid researcher recently counted the needles on a Christmas tree and found 296,140. He's working on an average needle count.

North America's tallest wooden flagpole is at the CNE in Toronto: it's 185 feet high. The pole was taken from a 300-year-old Douglas fir on Vancouver Island in 1977, and transported across Canada on three 62-foot-long flatcars.

The world's tallest known white elm towers 97 feet above Park Street in Dundas, Ontario. Its crown spread is 112 feet, its trunk up to 5 feet in diameter.

The oldest living plant seeds ever found were those of arctic lupines unearthed in 1954 in the Yukon. They had been dormant for more than 10,000 years.

The world's largest "tomato" is at Leamington, Ontario. It's actually an information booth, roughly 10 feet across and 25 feet high.

The only provincial floral emblem not native to Canada is Quebec's madonna lily, an immigrant from Europe and Asia.

Canada's largest tulip bed is in Ottawa, in front of the Parliament Buildings. It contains some three million tulips — enough to keep Pierre Trudeau in boutonnieres for more than 8,000 years.

RAILWAYS

The last spike of the CPR's trans-Canada railway was driven at Craigellachie, British Columbia, at 9:22 a.m. on November 7, 1885. There were actually *two* last spikes; the first bent after being struck several times and had to be replaced. The spike, however, was not made of gold or brass — but of iron.

The completed railway was 2,891 miles long. Stretching from Montreal to Port Moody, British Columbia, it was bound by some 30,527,900 spikes and 4,070,500 nuts, bolts and washers.

Canada's worst public transit system was probably the Red Line Transportation Company. During the winter of 1899 it operated a horse-drawn freight service across frozen Bennett Lake between Carcross and Bennett in the Yukon Territory. The conditions on the ticket read: "This pass is not transferable and must be signed in ink or blood by the undersigned person who thereby accepts and assumes all risks of damage to person and baggage. The holder must be ready to 'mush' behind at the crack of a driver's whip. Dewar Crown Scotch and Concha De Ragelias carried as sidearms are subject to inspection, and may be tested by officials of the road . . . . Passengers falling into the mud must first find themselves, and then remove the soil from their garments as the Red Line Transportation Company does not own the country . . . . No passenger is allowed to make any remarks if the horses climb a tree

The first domed observation railway car (with a raised deck enclosed by glass) was invented in Canada and used in the Rockies in 1896. It was withdrawn from service in 1897 — the sun turned it into an oven on wheels.

The first dining car, *The President*, was a combination kitchen-diner-sleeper developed in Canada and used on the Great Western Line in 1867.

The world's largest privately owned railway yards are in Winnipeg. Operated by Canadian Pacific, they cover two square miles and contain 338 miles of track — enough to accommodate 14,730 railway cars.

And for those who care about that sort of thing, Canada's first railway "hump yard" is located in Moncton, New Brunswick.

What is heralded as the world's biggest piggy bank is at Coleman, Alberta. Sometimes called "Ten Ton Toots" or "Dinky," the bank is actually an electric locomotive that was used in local mines. It was retired in 1954 and later given its present status — as a piggy bank for charitable contributions.

"Ten Ton Toots" isn't the only locomotive in Coleman. Another — complete with boxcars and caboose — lies at the bottom of nearby Crowsnest Lake. How did it get there? The train was

and each one must return to his seat if the sled drops through the ice, until the bottom of the lake is reached, when all are expected to get out and walk." And you thought Canadian National was bad?

The first locomotive in Canada was the *Dorchester*, built in 1836. It operated in Quebec between La Prairie and Saint-Jean.

During the 1880s Quebec had the world's only disappearing railway: tracks were laid across the frozen St. Lawrence between Longueuil and Montreal in November and taken up in April.

The world's first streetcar system was inaugurated at St. Catharines, Ontario, in 1887.

carrying illicit whiskey during Prohibition; it left the tracks shortly after the driver decided to test his cargo.

RELIGION

The "Biggest Little Church in the World" is in the Valley of the Dinosaurs near Drumheller, Alberta. The church is actually the smallest in Canada: no more than six worshippers at a time can fit into the 7-foot-wide, 12-foot-long structure. It has no regular congregation, no collection plate and no minister.

Niagara-on-the-Lake, Ontario, also claims Canada's smallest church, but actually it ranks only a close second. The church was built as a wayside prayer stop.

The only Islamic mosque in Canada and the first Islamic temple of worship in North America is the Mosque of Al Raschid in Edmonton. It was erected by Arabs who had come from desert homes to barter with Eskimos in the Arctic.

Canada's only stolen church is in Windermere, British Columbia. The story goes something like this: when residents of Donald, British Columbia, learned that they were to be relocated to Windermere, 80 miles away, and that their church was destined for Revelstoke, in the opposite direction, they were furious. So they stole the church. Dismantling it bit by bit, they smuggled it by rail and ferry to their new home. En route, however, the bell was stolen by an equally enterprising flock of Anglicans from Golden. Today the two churches bear witness to this strange turn of events: St. Peter's the Stolen is in Windermere, and St. Paul's of the Stolen Bell is in Golden.

The oldest church in Canada is Quebec City's Notre-Dame-des-Victoires. It was built in 1688, and later named in honor of French naval victories over British Admirals Phips and Walker.

Canada's only Mormon temple is at Cardston, Alberta. Dedicated on August 26, 1923, the octagonal structure of white granite is 148 by 148 feet. The largest stone in the building is a 10-ton block over the west entrance.

The biggest wooden church in North America is St. Mary's at Church Point, Newfoundland. It seats 750.

The world's highest granite spire is the 189-footer on St. Mary's Basilica in Halifax, Nova Scotia.

The most famous cross in Canada is almost certainly the 100-foot-high Mount Royal Cross overlooking Montreal. It is held together by 6,376 rivets.

During the mid-1850s Father Albert Lacombe held sway over the world's largest Roman Catholic parish: the entire Prairie region, an area of more than 680,000 square miles.

The first Canadian hymn, "We Love the Place O God," was written by W. A. Bullock in the late 1700s.

"What a Friend We Have in Jesus," one of the most famous hymns since David quit writing, was penned by Canadian Joseph Medlicott Scriven in Bewdley, Ontario, during the mid-1800s.

The oldest belfries in Canada are at the Shrine of Our Lady in Cap-de-la-Madeleine, Quebec. They date from 1694. The shrine also contains a painting of the Madonna. Three visitors who viewed it in 1888 swore they saw her eyes flicker momentarily.

The city in Canada with the most churches is Montreal. It has some 550 houses of worship, almost as many as Rome. This abundance once prompted Mark Twain to remark that "Montreal is the only city I know where you can't throw a brick without breaking a church window."

The most unusual steeple in Canada is probably the one on the Wilmot United Church in Fredericton, New Brunswick. At the spire's peak is a 12½-foot-high hand

with a 4-foot index finger pointing skyward. The meaning of the upright digit is open to interpretation.

Yes, Canada does have a patron saint: Saint Joseph. His feast day is March 19th, which — as you've probably noticed — goes uncelebrated.

What must be the oldest finger in Canada is a relic in the basilica at Sainte-Anne-de-Beaupré. It allegedly belonged to Saint Anne, the mother of the Virgin Mary, so we don't need to tell you how old the finger is.

Sainte-Anne-de-Beaupré, incidentally, is the Lourdes of Canada — since 1668 there have been some 350 documented cases of healings at the shrine. Each year roughly 660,000 faithful from around the world attend Mass there, 200,000 of them showing up for the July 26 Feast of Sainte-Anne.

The first Jewish resident of Canada was a woman — of sorts. Esther Brandeau spent almost a year with the Recollet monks at Quebec disguised as a man. Her real sex was discovered in 1740 and she was promptly kicked out of the country — not because she was a woman, but because Jews weren't permitted in New France.

Inuit thought early Christian missionaries had a screw loose: they couldn't understand what the preachers found so forbidding about an invitingly warm spot like Hell.

Canada's most unusual "saint" is Kateri Tekakwitha, one of the first Indian converts to Christianity in North America. Although not officially canonized by Rome, she is now patron saint of the pretzel, thanks to an organization called Pretzels for God (of which Kateri is spiritual leader). According to this group, the pretzel was originated by early Christians and symbolizes a person crossing his arms in prayer. Pretzels for God is not flourishing.

Canada's most bizarre religious group is the Sons of Freedom, a breakaway Doukhobor sect that believes destruction of material objects leads to spiritual salvation. In the past 50 years they have bombed or set fire to a hospital, three theaters, four post offices, four railway stations, eight churches, 22 villages, more than 50 sections of railway track, dozens of trains and hundreds of Doukhobor homes. They have destroyed grain elevators, stores, factories, some 20 sawmills, a bus station and a transmission tower — and they've touched off eight forest fires. Peter Verigin, a Doukhobor leader, was killed in 1924 when his train was bombed near Farron, British Columbia, allegedly by the Sons of Freedom. His tomb in nearby Castlegar has been blown up 11 times and the house of his grandson has been set ablaze more than half a dozen times.

The first YMCA in North America was founded in Montreal on December 9, 1851. There are now 77 main branches across Canada serving some 800,000 members. The YMCA originally limited membership to young men who "gave decided evidence of conversion to God."

RESTAURANTS, CLUBS & HOTELS

The oldest club in North America is the Order of Good Cheer, founded by Samuel de Champlain in 1606 at Port Royal, Nova Scotia. It is still in existence.

North America's largest restaurant is Ruby Foo's in Montreal. Its six dining rooms and several banquet halls seat more than 900 people. Each year the restaurant serves some 1,200,000 egg rolls, 825,000 pounds of spareribs, 150,000 pounds of red ribs and 95,000 pounds of short loins. And an ice-maker designed by the house engineer turns out about 1,300 cubes an hour.

The McDonalds outlet at the corner of Atwater and St. Catherine streets in Montreal set a North American record during the 1976 Olympics. It sold $74,000 worth of hamburgers in two weeks.

Since the first Canadian McDonalds opened in British Columbia in 1967, Canadians have become the world's biggest per capita consumers of burgers produced under the golden arches. The nation's 250-odd McDonalds franchises ring up annual sales of some $275 million (out of a worldwide total of $3 billion), and annual receipts here average about $860,000 per store compared to only $130,000 in the States.

Want to learn how to make a good burger? Try the McDonalds-operated Canadian Institute of Hamburgerology in Toronto.

The first Kentucky Fried Chicken outlet in Canada opened in 1958 in Saskatoon, Saskatchewan. Colonel Sanders' chicken empire spans 34 countries and sells seven million chickens a week.

One of the world's most unusual restaurants is co-owned by Quebec-born Bill Poulin. New York's Animal Gourmet caters to pets and has a menu that runs from shrimp cocktail to beef Wellington. It serves about 300 meals a week and provides birthday cakes and even flowers for a celebrating pet. Bill is a former lumberjack.

Canada's highest nightclub is Altitheque 727. It's located on the 42nd floor of Montreal's Place Ville Marie, 617 feet above the city.

North America's first discotheque, La Licorne, opened on Montreal's Mackay Street in 1961. Its owner, Gilles Archambault, had another first in October 1973. He unveiled La Sexe Machine — Canada's first bar with topless waitresses.

The only discotheque in the eastern Arctic is The Palace at Frobisher Bay. (A more appropriate location might have been nearby Disko Island.)

Canada's most classless hotel must have been the one operated by Alberta's Harry "Kamoose" Taylor back in the 1800s. House rules insisted that "all guests must rise at 6 a.m. as the sheets are needed as tablecloths." Who knows, maybe the spittoons doubled as soup bowls.

ROYALTY

Canada's only claimant to the British Crown is James III, who's alive and well and living in New Brunswick. He goes by the rather common appellation of Jim Stewart and his claim goes something like this: With the death of Bonnie Prince Charlie the crown of Scotland reverted to the heir of the second son of the first Stewart king, namely Robert, Earl of Fife. Fife's eldest surviving male descendant — hence rightful heir to the British throne — is James Alexander Stewart.

The only porridge pot in Canada that was owned by Bonnie Prince Charlie is in the Glengarry Pioneer Inn and Museum at Dunzegan, Ontario. It dates from 1746.

In 1943 part of Canada went Dutch — for a day. When Queen Juliana of the Netherlands gave birth to Princess Margriet in Ottawa's Civic Hospital the room was temporarily declared Dutch so the child could claim that country's citizenship.

SANITATION

Canada's most sophisticated outhouse, commonly dubbed the "Taj Mahal of Privies," is located at Kings Landing, New Brunswick. It's an elegant, eight-sided affair with windows, plastered walls and a 12-foot-high ceiling.

The only two-story outhouse in Canada is in Heritage Park, Calgary. It's attached to the Wainwright Hotel and patrons enter it by a raised catwalk.

Canadians use approximately 600 million rolls of toilet paper annually. In other words they use about 18 million miles of the stuff — almost enough to reach to the moon and back 37 times. The most-favored brand is Delsey.

Fortunately there are almost ten million household toilets in Canada. But to get an idea of how bad things *could* be, consider this: if everyone in Canada wanted to go to the same toilet at the same time, the line would stretch roughly 4,100 miles, and it would take almost nine years to get to the head.

The world's first flush toilet for cats was the invention of Vancouver's Doug Medly. The first flush toilet for *humans* is at the Minoan Palace at Knossos on Crete. It's about 4,000 years old.

What is reputed to be the world's largest collection of chamber pots is in Montreal's Cock n' Bull Pub. The oldest pot dates from 1855; Queen Victoria may have sat on it.

Canadians are one of the most wasteful peoples on earth: annually they throw out some 675 million tons of rubbish, including 3 billion bottles, 6.5 billion cans and 14 million worn tires. On the domestic scene, the average Canadian walks more than a mile and a half a year to dispose of garbage, and transports almost a ton of refuse in the process.

The cleanest place in Canada is a room in the Litton Systems industrial complex just outside Toronto. Called — not too imaginatively — the Super Clean Room, it maintains a dust-free level of 0.3 microns. In other words, any piece of dust larger than $1/250$ of the width of a human hair cannot get in — and neither can people with dandruff, flaking skin or ring-around-the-collar.

SCIENCE & INVENTIONS

The first Canadian patent was granted to William Hamilton on August 18, 1869, for his Eureka Fluid Meter, a device for measuring gasses and liquids. Canada's millionth patent was recorded on November 19, 1976 by Professor James Guillet and Dr. Harvey Troth, for Ecolyte, a plastic which self-destructs when exposed to sunlight.

The world's first automatic parliamentary desk-thumper was invented by Alex Wyse of Ottawa in late 1976. Energy (Wyse calls it hot air) from a speech is channeled through a mouthpiece and compressed in a cylinder which drives a mechanical arm attached to a wooden hand. Colored smoke accompanies the thumping: red for Liberals, blue for Conservatives and green for NDPs.

The paint roller was invented in 1940 by Norman Breakey of Toronto.

The zip fastener was invented by Gideon Sunback at St. Catharines, Ontario, in the 1940s. Since then, Sunback's fastener has zipped up everything from a patient's stomach (for easy post-operative access) to boots worn by sheep suffering from foot-and-mouth disease.

Canada's most ridiculous weapon is a pneumatic cannon that fires dead chickens at speeds of up to 600 miles an hour. Devised by the National Research Council, the cannon tests airplane parts likely to be struck by high-flying birds. Ammunition comes in two sizes: four-pound chickens for testing windshields, and eight-pounders for testing tail assemblies.

The world's fastest chicken-plucker — a whirring, mailbox-shaped contraption that can render a bird naked in about 30 seconds — was invented by Canadian Leonard Scheltgen in 1972.

The world's first washing machine was invented by a Canadian in 1824. Mr. Noah Cushing of Quebec City gets the credit.

And now here's Canada's brainiest food. In 1976 Ontario neurologist Dr. Adrian Upton thought he had discovered intelligent life in a Jello package. By attaching electrodes to a bowl of lime Jello he recorded wave activity similar to that of the human brain. A scientific breakthrough? No, the Jello wasn't thinking. It was simply vibrating in time with nearby machinery.

As early as 1685 Canada's first scientist, Michel Sarrazin, attempted to find an antidote for the effects of skunk spray. He failed.

SEX

Canada's noisiest lovemakers are humpback whales. During foreplay they slap each other with their flukes — a sound that carries for miles. Then they get down to business: they charge each other from about 1,000 yards, crash head-on and rise clamorously out of the water clutching each other for dear life.

The foulest hookers in Canadian history must surely have been some of the girls who flocked to the Klondike in 1898. Their names alone were enough to put you off sex for life: Deadeye Olga, Limping Grouse, Black Chicken and Sweetie the Pig were just a few. And then there was Six Bits, who once sold her favors for a gold nugget worth 85 cents.

The average Canadian penis is just that — very average. In the flaccid state it measures 3½ inches, which puts it in the running with French and West German penes, but makes it small stuff beside Swedish and Finnish penes: they average $5/12$ of a foot. None, however, can top the elephant's penis, which weighs an average of 60 pounds!

Canada's most ridiculous sex ordinance must be the one in Pictou, Nova Scotia, which makes it illegal to kiss any woman, *wife* included, on a Sunday.

Upper Canada in the early days offered an extreme example of Canadian modesty: it was illegal to hang men's and women's undergarments on the same washing line. Ladies' dainties were usually hung discreetly behind indoor screens.

Is there sex in Canada? According to statistics there is. The average Canadian male has sexual intercourse 1.19 times a week, the average female 1.18 times a week. What we can't figure out is this: while married men have sex 1.48 times a week, married women claim 1.57 times a week. Somebody must be cheating.

Canada's highest-paid stud is racehorse Northern Dancer. In 1976 a share of its breeding rights sold for $165,000. And judging from past performance, the horse earns its keep: in 1971, it studded 41 mares and sired 36 foals.

Canada's most widely unrecognized lover is probably John Robert Field, a Montreal hairdresser. In 1968 Field became an unwitting star of the film *Woodstock* when a camera caught him making love in the tall grass of upstate New York. He subsequently sued Warner Brothers for filming the nude

frolics, but it was barely worth the effort; he lost the case.

The world's most audacious streaker is Montreal's Michel Leduc. He trotted out among 500 dancing Catholic schoolgirls during the closing ceremonies of the 1976 Olympics — and was seen by a television audience of some two billion people.

During a local rape scandal, a Truro, Nova Scotia, newspaper quoted one policeman as saying: "We do all the rapes in Truro, and we haven't had any complaints lately."

The world's only herring sex sorter was designed by Vancouver's Neptune Dynamics to solve one of our greatest problems: how to tell the difference between a male and a female herring.

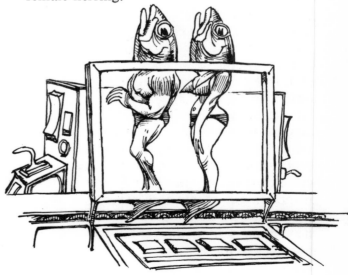

Canada's most unusual form of contraception was used by Bella Coola, Nootka and Coast Salish Indians. It was shredded bark and goat hair.

The world's only contraceptive museum is at the head office of Ortho Pharmaceutical (Canada) Ltd. in Don Mills, Ontario. Displays include camel contraceptives in vogue 3,000 years ago. To render the beasts pregnancy-proof, smooth pebbles were inserted into their uteri.

SMOKING

Canadians are the world's heaviest smokers. Some seven million smokers consume 64 billion cigarettes a year, discard roughly 174 tons of butts and empty packages daily and spend about $20,000 on cigarettes in a lifetime.

Quebecers, led by René Lévesque, are Canada's heaviest smokers: 64 percent of adult males and 40 percent of adult females partake of the weed.

It has been estimated that 250 Canadians a day — ten an hour — die from smoking. Latest findings show that tribes in Africa were smoking as long ago as A.D. 400, which certainly proves something — not one of those natives is alive today.

Finally, let's congratulate Air Canada. the national airline reserves 47.2 percent of all seats for nonsmokers.

Canada's biggest smoker is 1,245 feet high and weighs 38,390 tons. It's the world's tallest chimney, built by the International Nickel Company in Sudbury, Ontario.

At a news conference in March 1977 Prime Minister Trudeau was asked if he had ever smoked marijuana. "Do you mean inside or outside Canada?" he replied with a smile. "Someday I'll tell you about my travels."

The world record for match carving is held by Lindsay Gibson of Alameda, Saskatchewan. He notched 37 movable links in a standard wooden match — and left the head intact.

The world's biggest producer of wooden matches is the E. B. Eddy Company, established in Hull, Quebec, in 1851. The only remaining Canadian Allumettes Frontenac matchbox label — made by the company — is in Quebec City's Mrazik Collection.

SPORTS

One of Canada's most ludicrous sporting events was the great fox hunt in Barkerville, British Columbia, during the gold rush of 1865. It began when Clement Francis Cornwall, an English barrister, attempted to teach the noble sport to local prospectors. Sparing no expense, he purchased a manor house, imported a pack of English foxhounds, and dressed the rough-and-ready group in traditional hunting attire. He even trained an Indian named Henry to sound a silver horn. All that remained was to find a fox; there wasn't one, so an aging coyote was quickly substituted. One thing flawed what might have been a perfect hunt: Cornwall had difficulty getting the novices to shout "Tally-ho!" Every time they saw the coyote they forgot their instructions and whooped, "There goes the son of a bitch!"

Lacrosse is Canada's first national sport and North America's oldest organized sport. The world's only manufacturer of wooden lacrosse sticks (about 100,000 annually) is the Mohawk Company on Cornwall Island in Ontario.

If you thought hockey was Canada's number-one sport, think again. About one in three Canadians claim walking as their favorite sport (let's face it, almost everyone walks *somewhere*). Swimming ranks second, with one in five Canadians participating. And hockey? It places eighth; only one person in 20 participates.

The record for the number of goals scored in a world ice hockey match was set in 1947 when Canada shellacked a Danish team 47-0.

During regular season play, NHL goalies face more than 40,000 pucks. The league goes through about 15,000 pucks a year — enough to form a stack a quarter of a mile high.

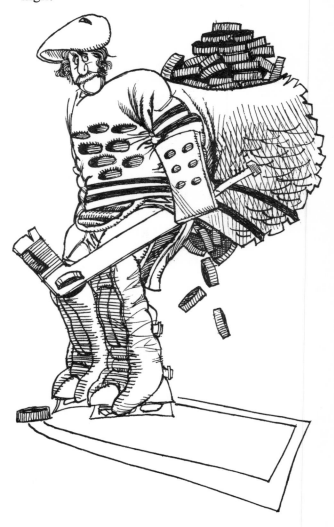

Canada's first hockey broadcast was carried by radio station CFCA from Toronto's Mutual Street Arena on March 21, 1923. Kitchener and Toronto Parkdale were playing. And the man at the mike? Foster Hewitt, naturally.

The largest sports audience in Canadian history viewed the Soviet Union-Team Canada game on September 11, 1976. CTV reported that 10,713,500 people, or 42 percent of Canada's population, tuned in.

The world's longest pro hockey game began on March 25, 1936, and didn't end until 2:25 a.m. on the 26th. After 2 hours 56 minutes of playing time the Detroit Red Wings scored a goal to defeat the Montreal Maroons in the sixth overtime period, 1–0. Officials had planned to end the marathon contest at the end of that period whether anyone scored or not.

The longest nonprofessional hockey game ever was played by 24 students from Calgary's Mount Royal College. They went at it nonstop for 56 hours 19 minutes 45 seconds in April 1971. The Pancakes trounced the Eagles 462-425.

Hockey's greatest comeback player was Mervin Dutton. Hit by exploding shrapnel during World War I, he took 48 metal fragments and his leg was mangled. Dutton refused to allow doctors to amputate the leg; instead he suffered 14 months with his leg hoisted at a 30° angle. But Dutton recovered and returned to play professional hockey — and serve a term as president of the National Hockey League.

The world's first official ice hockey champions were the Winnipeg Falcons, who won every game en route to the championship at the seventh Olympiad in Antwerp, in 1920.

Hockey's first streaker was Gilles Gratton. During a Toronto Toros practice in 1974 he skated several laps of the rink wearing nothing but skates and a goalie mask.

The fastest recorded puck speed is 118.2 miles an hour, posted by Bobby Hull with a left-handed slapshot. Hull is also hockey's fastest recorded skater. He was once clocked at almost 30 mph.

In an 1885 Montreal Winter Carnival hockey game, won by McGill University, the puck was neither rubber nor round. It was a two-inch cube of maple wood.

McGill also boasts Canada's oldest existing hockey stick, used by Lewis Skaife from 1878 to 1881.

The world's oldest skating champion was Joe Arsenault of Prince Edward Island. He won his last speed-skating trophy when he was 93 years old.

The longest skating rink in the world is Ottawa's Rideau Canal. A five-mile stretch of the waterway covers some four million square feet. It's maintained throughout the winter at an annual cost to taxpayers of some $50,000.

The largest artificial rink in the world is the 68,000-square-foot surface in Burnaby, British Columbia.

And the world's largest curling rink is Calgary's Big Four Rink: 96 sheets of ice that can accommodate 384 players.

The first ski lift in North America was built by Alec Foster and Jack Rabbit Johannsen at Shawbridge, Quebec, in 1922. They used an old automobile engine to power the lift and charged a nickel a tow.

North America's longest double chairlift is at Tod Mountain in Kamloops, British Columbia. The 9,413-foot lift makes a vertical ascent of 3,000 feet.

The world record for simultaneous somersaults on skis was established at Mont St. Sauveur, Quebec, in March 1977. Twenty-one skiers, all holding hands, did the flip.

The longest cross-country ski tour in the world is the Canadian Ski Marathon, a 100-mile wilderness trek from Lachute to Hull, Quebec. Recent competitors included a one-legged skier, a three-year-old, an octogenarian and a blind skier.

The world record for consecutive forward rolls is held by James Chelich of Fairview, Alberta. In September 1974 he executed 8,450 forward rolls over a distance of 8.3 miles, or one roll every five feet. Why, we're not quite sure.

Canada's premier ball-driver is Tad Aoki. In July 1977 the former Japanese black-belt judo champion dispatched 5,001 golf balls onto the fairway at a Vancouver course in only 12 hours.

Canada's longest hole-in-one was recorded by Phil Katsouris in May 1977. The Bois des Filion, Quebec, resident shot a 329-yard ace on the 12th hole of the St. Francis Golf Course. It was his first hole-in-one.

The only midnight golf tournament in the world is played each June at Yellowknife in the Northwest Territories.

The only golf club in the world where you can play *one* game in *two* countries is the Gateway Cities Golf Course, straddling the Saskatchewan-Montana border. Because the ninth hole is in two different time zones, it takes more than an hour to play — longer than any other hole in the world.

The Royal Montreal Curling Club, founded in 1807, is Canada's first curling club and the first sporting club of any kind in North America.

The Macdonald Brier Tankard championship, begun in 1927, is the world's largest curling event.

Basketball was invented in Canada long before the Globetrotters were a gleam in a coach's eye. 1891 was the year, and Dr. James Naismith of Almonte, Ontario, was the inventor. The "net" in the first game was a peach basket.

The Canadian record for nonstop basketball playing was set by students at Gloucester High School in Ottawa. In 1971 they played for 103 hours 14 minutes. Doug Publicover, the Gloucester team's top scorer, potted 647 points. But it went for nought: his side lost 3,426–2,411.

The finest women's basketball team in history was the Edmonton Grads. Losing only 20 of their 522 games, the Grads won the world championship in 1923 — and held on to it for 17 consecutive years before disbanding in 1940.

Canada's oddest sports team may have been the Ottawa Senators football club of the early 1920s. Protestant players refused to block for Catholic players. Catholics refused to block for Protestants. And neither would occupy the same players' bench. Yet in 1925 the team won the Grey Cup.

The first modern football game was played in May 1874 between Montreal's McGill University and Boston's Harvard University. It was in this game that the elongated football was first used. Harvard won, three touchdowns to none, but they were playing by U.S. rules and the Canadians had trouble adapting. The next day the teams played by Canadian rules; they tied.

The largest crowd in the history of Canadian team sport assembled at Montreal's Olympic Stadium on September 25, 1976: 68,505 spectators turned out to watch the Alouettes trim the Ottawa Roughriders 23-2.

The largest attendance at any Canadian sporting event, however, was the 933,777 people who visited the 1973 Calgary Stampede from July 5 to 14 (133,506 came on July 14 alone). These figures make the Stampede the world's largest rodeo.

Canada's most phenomenal attenance record is held by the Toronto Maple Leafs. They've sold out 16,307-seat Maple Leaf Gardens for every regular season game since 1946 — a total attendance of more than 34 million.

North America's oldest continuous sporting event is the St. John's Rowing Regatta in Newfoundland. The first record of the com–petition is dated 1828, but the regatta is believed to have begun some years earlier.

The world's longest rowing event is the Montebello Marathon, first held on May 22, 1977. The 42½-mile course runs from the Ottawa Rowing Club down the Ottawa River to Montebello, Quebec. Winner of the 14 entries was an eight from the University of Western Ontario, which covered the distance in 4 hours 39 minutes 38 seconds.

The world record for swimming the English Channel both ways was set by Toronto's Cindy Nicholas in September 1977. The 135-pounder swam the 45 miles from Dover, England, to Cap Gris Nez, France, and back, in just under 20 hours. The nonstop trip shaved 10 hours 5 minutes off the *men's* world record.

The only Canadian in history to win the world heavyweight boxing title was Tommy Burns (born Noah Brusso) from Hanover, Ontario. The 5-foot 7-inch, 175-pound scrapper was also the smallest person to do so, capturing the championship from Marvin Hart on February 23, 1906. Two years later Burns became winner of the *shortest* world heavyweight bout in history. He kayoed Jem Roche in 1 minute 28 seconds — 29 seconds less than the 1965 Muhammed Ali–Sonny Liston fight.

North America's oldest continuous turf event is the Queen's Plate. First held at Toronto's Carlton Track on June 27, 1860, the race is now run annually at Toronto's 780-acre Woodbine Race Track — the biggest racetrack in North America.

Mrs. Ralph Weir of Truro, Nova Scotia, created her own sport. In 1952, at age 52, she rocked in her chair for 93 hours 8 minutes, setting Canada's record for nonstop rocking.

Five-pin bowling was invented by Torontonian Thomas J. Ryan in 1909, but his game was tame compared to what must have been the most expensive bowling match in Canada. During the 1865 Cariboo gold rush a Major Downie used imported bottles of champagne for pins. And that was *ten*-pin bowling!

The most ridiculous ruling in professional Canadian sports was made in a 1941 baseball game. A Jersey City player batted, sending the ball along the base line while two runners scored. Montreal baseman Bert Haas waited for the ball to roll foul. When it didn't, he dropped to his knees and *blew* it foul. The umpire's ruling: fair play. The runs didn't count.

Canadians love their sport but most of them wouldn't know Karen Kain if they got tangled up in her leotards. About 3½ million spectators annually pay to watch sports events, yet only 165,000 go to the ballet.

STUNTS

The first person to go over Niagara Falls in a barrel and survive was a woman — Annie Edson Taylor. The 43-year-old schoolteacher performed the feat on October 24, 1901, becoming the unwitting founder of the exclusive "I Dood It" keg club. After her, six other daredevils attempted to duplicate the achievement. Only three were successful: Bobby Leach (1911), Jean Lussier (1928), and Nathan Boya (1961). Killed were Charles Stephens (1920), George Stathakis (1930), and William Hill Jr. (1951).

In the wake of her accomplishment, Ms. Taylor became involved briefly in theater, attempting to capitalize on her fame. She failed miserably: she was brave but boring. In a further effort to enliven her act she tried to salvage the historic barrel, which by then had rotted away. Using a phony keg, she took to street corners where she signed autographs and repeated her timeworn tale. She died at 63, penniless and alone, and was buried in a pauper's grave at Niagara Falls' Oakwood Cemetery.

Dozens of daredevils have attempted to conquer the falls. The most famous was Blondin, the celebrated tightrope walker who in 1859 crossed on four occasions, employing such props as a blindfold, a wheelbarrow and even a bicycle.

The only person to have survived the falls without a barrel was also the youngest: seven-year-old Roger Woodward, who took the plunge accidentally on July 9, 1960. He lost his running shoes in the process.

The world bare-handed brick-breaking champion is 132-pound Harold Warden of London, Ontario. He shattered 3,773 bricks in three hours.

The Canadian egg-tossing record is held by University of Saskatchewan student Lance Connell. He threw a fresh Grade A egg a distance of 223 feet 4 inches to classmate Everett Tromblay. The egg remained intact.

The holder of the world coin-tossing record is Chuck Biggs of Winnipeg. In February 1977 he piled 66 coins on his right elbow, snapped them into the air, and caught them with his right hand. The previous record catch was 65.

Canadians are among the happiest people in the world according to recent statistics — and this only helps to prove it: In 1976 Lisa Lester of Winnipeg broke the world record for smiling. The toothsome young miss won the Manitoba Dental Association's smilathon by grinning continuously for 10 hours 5 minutes, beating the previous world mark by almost 2½ hours.

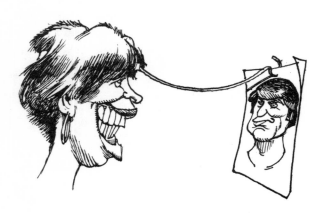

The Human Fly — a Montrealer who performs in a hood and jumpsuit and refuses to divulge his identity — set a world speed record for flying in open air on September 25, 1976. The Fly maintained a speed of 250 miles an hour for 26 minutes while secured to the outside of a DC-8 cruising at 4,000 feet above California. A thunderstorm foiled his bid to hit 300 mph — he suffered severe injuries from, of all things, raindrops.

A Canadian car-stuffing record was set by students at Glengarry Secondary School in Hamilton, Ontario: 111 kids squeezed into and onto a parked Volkswagen.

The Canadian record for automobile occupancy (interior only) was established in Candiac, Quebec, in March 1977 when 19 students crammed into a Volkswagen Beetle.

The longest underwater submergence without a diving bell ever recorded was made by Toronto's Patrick Morrison and Americans Joe Mangus and Alberta Jones. In 1961 they stayed under for more than five days.

Canada's wackiest acupuncture treatment was attempted in the spring of 1977 by Lowell Darling. The self-proclaimed therapist stuck a five-foot wooden needle into radio station CFRO, the "ear" of Vancouver, in an attempt to combat the

city's heroin-addiction problem.

It was not Darling's first foray into creative medicine. He claims to have nailed down most of the western world's biggest cities so they won't slide off the earth from the weight of overpopulation. And he has laced up sections of California's San Andreas Fault with rawhide to prevent another earthquake like the one in 1971.

But what may have been Darling's most outrageous idea was never put to use. During U.S. nuclear testing in 1971, when Canadian fears about the effects of radioactive fallout were most intense, he wrote Prime Minister Trudeau with a solution. He suggested Canada build 40 story electric fans along the Canada-U.S. border to repulse radiation, and a plexiglass shield along our northern frontier to protect the south from subsequent arctic drafts. Trudeau's office rejected the plan — it claimed the scheme would "leave Canada in a vacuum."

WEATHER

The first Canadian weather forecast was made in 1871, the year the National Meteorological Service was established.

The best year-round weather in Canada occurs at Sumas, British Columbia. The area has a mean daily temperature — including nighttime and winter readings — of 11°C (51.6°F).

Canada's highest temperature was recorded at Gleichen, Alberta: the thermometer registered 46°C (115°F) — and that was in the shade.

The lowest temperature ever recorded in Canada was –63°C (–81°F). The cold snap hit Snag River in the Yukon on February 3, 1947 — the day after Groundhog Day.

The record rainfall in Canada occurred at Henderson Lake, British Columbia in 1931. That year it received some 320 inches.

Canada's sunniest spot is Sachs Harbour, Northwest Territories. In June 1958, it averaged more than 17½ hours of sunshine a day.

The coldest — and windiest — street corner in Canada is reputed to be Winnipeg's Portage and Main. Winter temperatures there hover at –40°C (–40°F) for days on end, and fierce winds make the spot even less inviting.

Canadian Bob Gauchie survived arctic conditions longer than any other human when his plane went down north of the Arctic Circle in 1967. He was subjected to temperatures of –51°C (–60°F) for 58 days before being rescued.

Gauchie's plane, incidentally, was repaired and flown home. Seven months later it crashed again and the pilot and four passengers were killed. This time, however, Gauchie wasn't on board.

Canada's record snowfall occurred at Mount Copeland, British Columbia. In 1971-72 it received 963 inches of snow. Ranger Station, Alberta, holds the record for Canada's greatest one-day accumulation of snow: 44 inches.

Canada's highest snow removal costs are in Outremont, a Montreal suburb. The community yearly spends an average of $33,000 per mile — or 50 cents an inch.

Canada's foggiest province is Newfoundland, and the foggiest place in the world is Grand Banks, Newfoundland. The region is socked in an average of 120 days a year.

ZOOS

The first North American zoo north of Mexico was founded in 1847 at Halifax by Andrew Downs. It folded 21 years later.

North America's largest zoo is the 710-acre Metro Toronto Zoo. Each month its animals gobble up about $20,000 worth of food. The menu includes 4,000 live crickets, 100 pounds of fish, 200 pounds of horsemeat and 125 pounds of fruit and vegetables — a day.

The Canuck Book can be
expanded and revised almost
endlessly, and with this in
mind, we hope to prepare a
second and enlarged edition.
But we need your help. If you
know of something worth
including in the next volume —
something bigger, better,
odder, older — drop us a line.

Ian Walker   Keith Bellows

P.O. Box 527
Westmount
4225 Ste. Catherine W.
Montreal, Que. H3Z 2T5